HAPPILY MARRIED FOREVER

HAPPILY MARRIED FOREVER

by Natalie Tyler
Edited by John Tyler

Harmony Publishers

INTERNATIONAL STANDARD BOOK NO. 0-9702381-0-X
LIBRARY OF CONGRESS CARD NO. 00-108453

HAPPILY MARRIED FOREVER
Tyler, Natalie

Copyright ©2001, Natalie Tyler
All rights reserved.
Printed in USA.

No part of this book may be reproduced, stored in a retrieval system, or transmitted, in any form or by any means, electronic, mechanical, photocopying, microfilming, recording or otherwise, without written permission from the authors.

Portions from A Course in Miracles, © 1975, 1992, 1999, reprinted by permission of the Foundation for A Course in Miracles, 1275 Tennanah Lake Road, Roscoe, NY 12776-5905. The ideas represented herein are the personal interpretation and understanding of the authors and are not necessarily endorsed by the copyright holder of A Course in Miracles®.

Cover Design & Illustration © 2001 by Karen Bacon
Cover Photographs by Paradise Photography
Harmony Publishers

"You have slept

for millions and millions of years.

Why not wake up this morning?"

—Kabir

Dedication

I dedicate this book to Frances "Hutch" Tyler (1907-1998), for bringing up your son to be such a nurturing, sensitive, loving, wise, playful, deep man, who is my ideal husband, co-therapist, editor, playmate, and stimulating, adventurous, intellectual, cosmopolitan at home anywhere travel companion; to all of our couple therapy clients who have taught us so much on their journey to a conscious marriage; to our son, Jonathon Berliner, for teaching us so much about courage and forgiveness; to the memory of our son, Joey Berliner (1959 – 1994); to my mentor, Robert Goulding, M.D. (1917 – 1992); to all of our other children: Jeff & Michelle, Jill, Burr & Eron, Beth & Lloyd, Cassie; and all of our grandchildren.

Acknowledgments

I wish to give special appreciation to dear friend, mentor and teacher, Mary Goulding, MSW (along with her great husband and co-therapist, Robert Goulding, M.D. who passed on in 1992), for teaching me how to have fun changing lives creatively with Transactional Analysis-Gestalt-Redecision Therapy. I'll always cherish those transforming experiences on The Mountain at the Western Institute for Group and Family Therapy—your friendship, your politics (how nice to have such a brilliant friend who agrees with me!) And the fun I have laughing with you at conferences and workshops, and during your snorkeling visits here on Maui (may there be many more!)

We are grateful to Harville Hendrix, Ph.D., author of *Keeping The Love You Find*, for creating IMAGO Therapy (how much easier it is to teach couples how to heal each other using those tools!), and for many of the concepts in Chapter 3 (Stages of Relationship), Chapter 4 (Conscious Marriage), and Chapter 7 (Caring Behaviors). Thanks to Virginia Satir for the Daily Temperature Reading, to George Bach for the Hair Cut, Vesuvius, and Fair Fight for Change, and to Wayne Dyer, Ph.D., for his insights and spiritual depth.

Mahalo nui loa* to Dr. Jerry Jampolsky for our time together immediately before my cancer operation, for bringing *A Course in Miracles* to a brighter light for me, and for teaching me the true meaning of forgiveness. Because of Jerry—the enlightened being he is, his face, his eyes, his smile, his heart, his advice, and how completely he allows Spirit to flow through his healing work—my healing was easy, complete and forever.

Mahalo to Linda Ion and her wonderful husband,

---

*Hawaiian for "Thank you very much."

Ted, who passed on this year, for all your computer help with the manuscript, to Pam Stuart for cleaning up after all the mess while I wrote, and to my comrades in the Maui Live Poets Society and Poetopia for vigorously applauding our poems.

An extra grandmotherly "Mahalo" with deep Aloha to granddaughter Amanda for your sensitivity, appreciation, and independence during the summer of my cancer challenge. A special "Mahalo" with deep Aloha to granddaughter Shanti for all the healing laughs, and for chasing away the bogeymen during that cancer summer. You two singing angels gave my heart the spirit to heal and finish this book. Mahalo for visiting your Tutu* during that and all the other important summers!

I am grateful to my spiritual sister, Lois Janis, for reading parts of my manuscript and for your encouragement and feedback; to Le Claire Taylor for your support and encouragement just when I needed it most; to Judy Grimes for your friendship and spiritual guidance.

Thanks to the Maui Crones for being exactly who you are and including me, and to my beloved Unity family.

A very special "thank you" to my son, Jonathon Berliner, for all the strokes and laughter. And finally, thanks to my dear clients, and to the Tuesday afternoon WOW—Wild Outrageous Women—Group for our deep heart connection and mind expansion and for the love.

I could not have written this book without the Maui Writers Conference and Retreat. Thanks to Shannon & John Tullius for your loving work, and to Bud Gardner, Dan Poynter and Jack Canfield for the expert education, mentoring and motivation I received. And thanks to Victor Pellegrino for the publishing advice and help with the production of the book.

Mahalo nui loa to my husband, Blue Rivers, for

*Hawaiian for Grandma

patiently—sometimes late at night—taking all my scribble-scrabble and organizing it on his magical computer—*and never complaining.* "Blue Rivers" was bestowed upon John by a kahuna* during a strange magical afternoon.—Natalie

Mahalo to my wise brothers, the Sages, for your consistent support and our deep Saturday afternoons together. Mahalo nui loa to my wife, Munira—Healer with Light—for being the most creative woman I've ever known or imagined. The door sign I gave her for Christmas says: "A wild, wise, wacky, wonderful woman lives here," and it's true! Natalie received the name "Munira" (Healer with Light) from Sufi teacher Pir Vilayat Inayat Khan after he witnessed her doing therapy at Omega Institute in Rhinebeck, New York.—John

*Hawaiian for spiritual teacher

Contents

Introduction   13
Mise en Scene   17

Part I: Love—What's It All About?

1. What Love Really Is   23
2. The Difference Between Codependent Addiction & Lasting Deep Love   37
3. Stages of Relationship   51
4. Conscious Marriage   71

Part II: How to Do It

5. He Says, She Says—Loving Communication   91
6. Closer Through Conflict   111
7. Caring Behaviors   131
8. Sexuality & Sensuality—or My Secret Fabulous Life in Paradise   141
9. Keeping the Spark Alive   175
10. Forgiveness   181
11. Vintage Love—Growing Older—and Younger!—Together   203

Part III: Everything Else You Need to Know

12. Healthy Happy People, Healthy Happy Couples, Healthy Happy Families   221
13. Conscious Parenting   239
14. Back to the Beginning—Living Together   263
15. Marriage Commitment   271
16. Blended Families   277

Epilogue   281
Appendices   285
Citations to A Course in Miracles   301
Bibliography   303

Introduction

THIS BOOK, WHY I WROTE IT AND HOW TO USE IT

"Some books are to be tasted, others to be swallowed, and some few are to be chewed and digested."
—Francis Bacon

"Camerado, this is no book. Who touches this, touches a man."
—Walt Whitman
(*A woman*, in this case, Walt. —Natalie)

Dear Reader,

Thank you for buying or borrowing this book. I write from all the wisdom I have gathered over the years from trials and tribulations, my clients, our Happily Married Forever couples, our PAIRS® (Practical Application of Intimate Relationship Skills) couples, the transformed families John and I have loved counseling, the many teachers, spiritual mentors, master therapists, workshops, psychological conferences, spiritual retreats, three Maui Writers Conferences and two Maui Writers Retreats, and my reading habit. Sometimes I read all day at the beach to the sound of the surf, sometimes all night to the fragrance of night blooming jasmine, gardenias and ginger outside my window. Mark Twain once said, "The man who does not read good books has no advantage over the man who cannot read them." And Sir Richard Steele said, "Reading is to the mind what exercise is to the body."

I have learned the most from my own marriage, and my wise, good, loving husband. As Charles Dickens said, "A loving heart is the truest wisdom."

I suggest reading Part I, Chapters 1, 2, 3, and 4, discussing them with your partner, and digesting the ideas. The love poems can be read aloud to each other, and you might be inspired to write some of your own! The exercises in Part II, Chapters 5, 6, 7 and 10, are for using everyday. If you're ready for some hot nights in the old town of Conscious Loving, read Chapter 8. If you're skeptical or need inspiration, read our love story in Chapter 11, Vintage Love—Growing Older—and Younger!— Together. Parents—hey—go right to Chapters 12 & 13, especially if you're blessed with the challenge of living with teenagers. My favorite chapters in order are: Chapter 11: "Vintage Love"; Chapter 8: "Sexuality & Sensuality"; and Chapter 1: "What Love Really Is." Read the chapters in any order you choose. It's your book now! Life is decisional! You're free!

I don't believe in exclusiveness, or that some of us are more important than others, so I'm alternating pronouns. In one chapter I'll say "she" and "her", and the next "he" and "him", so kindly use your imagination and know I mean you and the Dear One who is the most important person in your life. I also believe each person has a right to love whomever they please, and I've written this book for all those who love: straight, gay, and lesbian. Love whomever you choose, but love!

If you've been married a long time, I invite you to use this book as the miracle you need for renewal just at the right time! If you're in a new relationship, and you've discovered this book, read it together. Coincidences are God's way of remaining anonymous. If you're single, this is the time to read this book and learn, so you can start out right when love comes a-knockin'. Rainer Maria Rilke wrote: "The more one is, the richer is all that one experiences. And whoever wants to have a deep love in his life must collect and save for it and gather honey."

Ralph Waldo Emerson said: "We become what we think about all day long." As I walk on the golden beach

INTRODUCTION 15

here on my beloved Maui; as I snorkel and meditate on the electric blue, yellow striped, iridescent violet, orange-tailed and pastel plaid fish; as I do my work of helping couples to heal and enrich their relationships; I am also on a deep level feeling grateful for my darling husband and this marriage, even better than I ever imagined a marriage could be. The universe has rewarded me magnificently for using the pain of my childhood and early adult years to learn and to keep growing and to forgive the past. I believe what the Zen parable teaches: "Now that my house has burned down, I have a much better view of the sky." I have forgiven the mother who didn't know how to love me, the husband I married hoping I'd finally win her approval (but never did), and all the others from my past. They did what they knew how to do given their limitations and the conditions of their lives. Everyone who came into my life was a teacher to me. As Wayne Dyer says, "I am grateful to all those people who said no. Because of them, I did it myself."

I have stretched and through my conscious marriage to Sir Tallness (same husband—different pet name), I have transformed my life. To quote Wayne Dyer again, "Transformation is the ability and willingness to live beyond your form instead of living in a world of limitations."

Writing this book is my way of saying "Thank you" for all the treasures in my life, and to all the clients who taught me so much during our journey together in individual therapy, couple therapy, family therapy, and our couples workshops. As Bill Moyers said, "In their own way, all of the men and women with whom I talked are the teachers. Sharing is the essence of teaching. It is, I have come to believe, the essence of civilization."

The names of the people in the vignettes throughout this book, and the clients, students, and friends I've quoted, have either given me permission to use their names, stories and words, or I've changed the names to protect the guilty!

Jeanne Moreau said, "Life is tough enough without being unhappy on top of everything else!" and Abraham Lincoln said, "People are about as happy as they make up their minds to be."

If you read this book carefully, digest the philosophy, and use the tools on a regular, daily basis, you too can achieve *Heaven* in a transforming, blissful relationship. As I write this book, I'm expanding my overflow to all who read these words, and to those who don't. I invite you to open your mind and heart and stretch to digest what you read, do the exercises with your partner, and breathe the love in and out.

"Man's mind stretched to a new idea never goes back to its original dimensions."—Oliver Wendell Holmes

"I'm a great believer in luck, and I find the harder I work, the more I have of it."—Stephen Leacock

"If you asked me what I came in this world to do, I will tell you. I came to live out loud."—Emile Zola

"I have never quite believed that one chance is all I get. Writing is my way of making other chances."—Anne Tyler

Again and again, one more time (for now), thank you, Cap'n Easy—same husband—I've given him so many nicknames, and he deserves them all. What wizards do by magic, he does by goodness, love, and courage.

Now get comfortable, put your feet up, find a sensuous, flowing red or green or purple pen for underlining, get a crispy apple or snack of your choice—did I hear chocolate? —and *voila!* Have fun, stimulate your mind and be happy.

John Masefield says, "The hours that make us happy make us wise."

Mise En Scene

On this island of Maui, in the land of rainbows and endless summer, people honor the custom of taking off their shoes before entering anyone's sacred home or office; the children call the adult women Auntie—and we all look after them at social gatherings; the fireworks on New Year's Eve last longer than the 4th of July; and the dinner parties start at five o'clock, so we can see each other's gardens and watch the sunset before dark. We awaken to bird songs in the mornings, instead of alarm clocks. There don't seem to be enough hours in the day. As dear son, Jonny, said when he and his friend left soon after our Jambalaya dinner last night, "It gets late early here, doesn't it?" Time seems to float in a different dimension in our life here on this magnificent, wildly colorful, enormous green rock in the middle of the ocean.

One day as I was strolling along Keawakapu Beach, I came upon a friend walking toward me from the opposite direction. Richard said, "Do you think we've all died and gone to heaven, and we just don't know it?" I think heaven is like Maui except with no traffic or shopping centers, and even more book stores, libraries, Hawaiian music and chants, Thai, Vietnamese, Indonesian, Indian, and Chinese restaurants replacing all the little tourist trap trinket stores. Of course, in Heaven we'd still have all these beaches, the vast ocean, and all the whales and dolphins to play with.

This is the island—and these are the people—who have inspired me to live this good life, and to write this good book. I give it to you with my deepest Aloha.

HAPPILY MARRIED FOREVER

PART I

LOVE—
WHAT'S IT ALL ABOUT?

1

What Love Really Is

"Everything has to do with loving and not loving."
—Robert Bly—

July 4th—tonight my one and only true love and I celebrate the anniversary of the night we began our life together, and the birthday of our country. We feel blessed that every year the entire population of the United States of America helps us celebrate, with fireworks lighting up the old black magic sky. We remember the night he flew in from a California trip (he was living in New York then) in time to watch the fireworks with me in the balmy western Massachusetts sky. He came for the weekend to share the sparkling celebration, and he never left, and we've never stopped celebrating! Our life together has been spectacular fireworks ever since (some days are loud bangs, many nights are gentle sparklers, and others are overhead iridescent colors of green, purple, red and blue silvery hues coming down in showers upon us.) At the magic hour right before dusk here on Maui, in that special golden light that precedes sunset, we board the Wailea Kai, and sail into the ocean to watch The Show. We have fun singing "Loving in the Light" and other Hawaiian love songs. Finally we eat our Hawaiian barbecued fish with beans and rice and pineapple slaw, as we watch the brilliant red sun pass over the West Maui Mountains and slowly sink into the sea between Lahaina and Lanai. As the sun drops below the horizon, the many fluffy small clouds transform into pink surprises lined with Maui gold. The afterglow of violet and lavender and smoky gray transports my mind into thoughts and hopes and even plans of how our night might end when we are at home alone. I gaze at the sky, then at the handsome face of this man who has chosen me above all others to share this holy night and this glorious life.

We're sitting on the bow with new friends Pam and Dick, fresh from Montana. Dick says, "Everyone here on Maui is so wonderful. Were you this wonderful before you moved here?" "We weren't so wonderful until we met each other," answers my Cap'n Easy.

We anchor the boat about 300 yards from shore near the fireworks barge. Suddenly, sounds of celebration! Extravagant fountains of icy green, silvery purple, electric blue, brilliant pink, flaming red, luminous silver and iridescent gold, with streams of white stars, shimmer into the dark night sky and shower into the mysterious ocean.

All the way back to Maalaea Harbor, we gaze at millions of bright stars overhead, and we all smell the gardenias in my hair, picked by this lover pal of mine from the overflowing, shiny green foliage outside my office. In the car on the way home, we listen to the holy music of Ella Fitzgerald singing, "I give myself in sweet surrender to my one and only love." Finally at home we're welcomed by the wild jungle scent of night-blooming jasmine along our walk as we enter our peaceful miniature castle on the hill. We're under the spell of this

© Mel Lazarus. Reprinted with Permission

WHAT LOVE REALLY IS

magical night. Our eyes tell each other more than our sleepy murmurings. Our bodies sing a melody of love.

WHAT IS LOVE?

This is the question most often asked by clients and friends. The brave people who have asked these questions have come to us for therapy, coaching, or to learn the answers they didn't learn in school and haven't found in books. Some of these pioneers come to us to decide whether to divorce or stay married. Some travel this exciting road with us to decide whether to marry or stay single, or whether to take the risk of opening their hearts, or whether to break up with a lover because the relationship isn't perfect like the childhood fantasies were.

Every spiritual teacher, from Jesus to Mother Theresa, has stated the answer simply: to love one another is to offer pardon where there is hatred and help where there is need. It is quiet understanding, mutual confidence, sharing and forgiving. It is loyalty through the good times and bad. It settles for less than perfection and makes allowances for weakness. Love is content with the present, it hopes for the future, and it does not brood over the past. It is the day-in, day-out chronicle of irritations, problems, compromises, small disappointments, big victories and common goals. Over a hundred years ago, Sir James Barrie said, "If you have it, you don't need to have anything else, and if you don't have it, it doesn't matter what else you have."

Love is feeling even better about ourselves when we're with our beloved than we do at other times. Love is caring so much about our partner that we put energy, time and enthusiasm into caring behaviors, not for the purpose of "making him love me more," but for his happiness and delight. Love feels safe, comfortable, non-demanding, unobtrusive, and non-judgmental, and at times fun, exciting and energizing. In love, giving and receiving are the same, and giving feels as heart warming as receiving. Love is giving each other the gift of time, and putting each other first above all others. It's about staying conscious about the other person's needs, wounds, preferences and sensitivities. Love is relishing spending long hours alone together with no need to talk, spending long hours together sharing ideas, feelings, dreams, and past experiences without defensiveness. Love is long hours of touching, caressing and kissing with no goal in mind. In love, laughter and tears are shared freely, and we feel so much overflow that it is easy to pour our overflow out to others.

When asked to define what love is, people in various studies have ranked trust, loyalty, commitment, honesty, and friendship as the most important elements, followed by nurturing, respect, shared fun, shared values and affection.

Love is the way we live our lives together, sharing disappointments, joy, nature, poetry, laughs, music, friends, children and grandchildren. Love is long hours of loving touches and communicating our feelings and thoughts, knowing we won't be judged by the other. Love is listening carefully to each other. It is appreciating, acknowledging, complimenting and affirming each other verbally. It is daily caring behaviors, high energy fun, and surprising each other often.

We live our love by remembering to praise each other in private and in public, and to make requests for change without criticism. We stay conscious by remembering that the purpose of marriage is to heal each other's wounds and make closure with childhood. We nurture our marriage by making each other and our relationship the top priority.

Love, the state of being and doing, can fully transform energy, as it is an exchange of energy. Protective circles cut off energy. We need to stop protecting ourselves from love and drop everything that is not love, and

WHAT LOVE REALLY IS 27

then we will know what love is. When Michelangelo was asked how he sculpted such magnificent works of art, he said, "I simply chip away everything that is not the statue." We need to follow that beautiful example, and remove the blocks to the awareness of love's presence. Love is our essence, and our task is to chip away everything that is *not* love, including judgments, criticism, blame, and uncaring behaviors.

Love is a sacred path, which enables us to know more fully who we are and what is important in life. Love allows us to cultivate the fullness and depth of who we are and what life is about. When we truly love one other person fully, then we can love all beings on this planet. Once we open our hearts fully to one other person, the veil lifts, the spirit soars, and a whole new world of wonders opens to us.

Reprinted with Permission, Mister Boffo © Joe Martin
Distributed by Universal Press Syndicate

The icing on the cake of love is that it is the key to our spiritual growth. It provides us with great opportunities to learn our life lessons. In consistently choosing love, we experience a personal transformation, which leads us to join rather than separate from those around us.

Deep lasting spiritual love takes many years to develop. It happens when both people let go of wanting the other to change, and they each accept imperfections with tenderness. It happens when we feel and express gratitude for being so fortunate to be loved.

HOW DO I KNOW IF I AM REALLY IN LOVE?

This is a familiar second question we often hear from many of our clients and students. One answer comes from Robert A. Johnson, who wrote, "Love is content to do many things that the ego is bored with. Love is willing to work with the other person's moods and unreasonableness."

Here are some questions that will help you find answers:
• Do you feel better about yourself when you are with your beloved?
• Do you put her happiness above needing to be right?
• If you were not in love would you choose this person to be your best friend?
• Does she make you want to be a better person?

If you answered yes to these four questions, you'll probably know if yours is real love by the end of this book, especially if you read it together. If the answers are no, please be sure to part as friends, or call your friendly neighborhood therapist.

Dr. Howard Halpern says, "A love relationship implies commitment to the other's well being, not destructive behavior. There is no love relationship without kindness, protectiveness and mutual respect. Being in a love relationship without the feelings of being in love can be deadening. Feeling in love without a loving relationship can be deadly. Being in love within a love relationship is a blessing."

SO MANY TIMES I'VE THOUGHT I WAS IN LOVE AND IT TURNED SOUR. I DON'T KNOW IF I'VE EVER SEEN OR EXPERIENCED LOVE. HOW IS IT DIFFERENT FROM ALL THE CRUSHES I'VE HAD?

This is usually the next question, and it's a great question! Chapter Two is all about the difference between co-dependent addictive crushes and lasting Deep Love! We'll get to that in a few minutes.

In the meantime I invite you to take into your mind and heart Eric Butterworth's expression, "Love is not finding the right partner, it is being the right partner." In healthy love partners are interdependent rather than co-dependent. They both feel full and complete; they want the other person's energy and attention, but they don't need it. They accept each other as they are and don't try to change the other. They concentrate on being the best possible person and partner. A healthy lover feels that "you make me want to be a better person because I'm with you." In lasting authentic love, partners accept each other's imperfections and stretch to heal each other's wounds. They consider their own happiness and their partner's happiness on an equal basis. They prefer their spouse's time, energy and attention, and they are not attached to needing to have it. Love that lasts is between equals who sometimes put the other's preferences above their own; who never purposely hurt each other; and who consciously protect each other's hearts.

I DON'T THINK MY PARENTS SEEMED TO BE IN LOVE. CAN PEOPLE STILL FEEL DEEP EXCITING LOVE AFTER THEY HAVE BEEN MARRIED FOR MANY YEARS?

This is another frequently asked question, so we've written a whole chapter for you on Vintage Love—Growing Older—and Younger! —Together, Chapter 11. Feel free to read it now. You don't have to read these chapters in order. It's O.K., really.

I will tell you one thing: after all these years, I still like, love, admire, respect, cherish and adore my husband, and this is my favorite decade! Yes. Yes. Yes.

Are you in love? Are you convinced? Do you want to

hear more? Take off your shoes—we don't wear them on Maui—put up your feet, put on soft music, prepare a snack of your choice, and read these next pages aloud with your Sweetheart. Margaret Atwood says, "The Eskimos had fifty-two names for snow because it was important to them: there ought to be as many for love." I offer you a few of the beautiful, creative words that wise and famous people have used to describe love:

"Love is patient, love is kind and is not jealous; love does not brag and is not arrogant, does not act unbecomingly; it does not seek its own, is not provoked, does not take into account a wrong suffered, does not rejoice in unrighteousness, but rejoices in truth; bears all things, believes all things, endures all things. Love never fails."
—1 Corinthians 13: 4-8

"Love is an act of choice, will and effort that involves extending oneself for the sake of another, whether or not one feels loving at the moment. Love is the will to extend one's own self for the purpose of nurturing one's own and another's spiritual growth."—M. Scott Peck

"The purpose of intimacy is to massage the heart, to soften the muscles around our hardened places and keep pliant the place where we are already open. The circle of love is deep and strong. It can forgive mistakes and cast out error. It can foster greatness and bring forth new life. There is nothing it cannot do. Love is God."
—Marianne Williamson

"Don't you think I was made for you?" Zelda Fitzgerald asked F. Scott Fitzgerald shortly after they met. "I feel like you had me ordered and I was delivered to you."

"Love is an act of will, a decision to commit my life completely to that of the other person."—Eric Fromm

WHAT LOVE REALLY IS

"Love does not consist in gazing at each other, but in looking outward together in the same direction."
—Antoine De Saint-Exupery.

"You're not sick, you're just in love."—Irving Berlin

"Love cures people ... both the ones who give it and the ones who receive it."—Dr. Karl Menninger

"Love is not a feeling but a verb, and an active verb at that."—Jerome Travers, Ph.D.

"A coward is incapable of exhibiting love; it is the prerogative of the brave."—Gandhi

"The loving are the daring."—Bayard Taylor

"For one human being to love another: that is perhaps the most difficult task of all ... the work for which all other work is but preparation. It is a high inducement to the individual to ripen ... a great exacting claim upon us, something that chooses us out and calls us to vast things."—Rainer Maria Rilke

"The risk to love is the risk to become vulnerable. We can only love if we risk being hurt."—Barry & Joyce Vissell

"Love is a metaphysical gravity."
—R. Buckminster Fuller

"People think love is an emotion. Love is good sense."—Ken Kesey

"Neither a lofty degree of intelligence, nor imagination, nor both together go to the making of genius. Love, Love, Love, that is the soul of genius."
—Wolfgang Amadeus Mozart

"The Commitment of Love: Love endures only when lovers love many things together and not merely each other."—Walter Lippmann

"A lover does not figure the odds."—Jelaluddin Rumi

"Greater joy will come to us through love than in any other way." —Betty Eadie

"We have laughs together. I care about you. Your concerns are my concerns. We have great sex."
—Character in the film "Manhattan."

"To fear love is to fear life. Love is the basis of all life."—Bertrand Russell.

"There is no remedy for love but to love more."
—Henry David Thoreau

"Love is, above all, the gift of oneself."—Jean Anovilh

"Send two dozen roses to Room 424 and put 'Emily, I Love You' on the back of the bill."—Groucho Marx

"I have seen the truth. It is not as though I had invented it with my mind. I have seen it, SEEN IT, and the living image of it has filled my soul forever ... In one day, one hour, everything could be arranged at once. THE CHIEF THING IS TO LOVE." —Fyodor Dostoyevsky

"A bell is not a bell till you ring it. A song is not a song till you sing it. Love was not put into your heart to stay. Love is not love till you give it away."
—Oscar Hammerstein's last written words

"Love, which created me, is what I am." [1]
—A Course in Miracles

"Do the best you can in the place where you are and be kind."—Scott Nearing.

"Do not worry about breaking your heart. Break open the wall around your heart—the defensive shield you have constructed to protect yourself from loving and being loved fully. Love is a decision—an act of will translated into action ... a life orientation to be a loving person."—John Welwood

"The feeling of being in love requires only one person; a love relationship requires two. A love relationship requires high degrees of mutual sharing, caring, respect and involvement. The feeling of being in love is not enough to support a love relationship."
—Dr. Howard Halpern

"Love is a friendship that has caught fire."
—Jeremy Taylor

"The challenge of love is an invitation to surrender all our masks and pretenses and to wake up to our own innate wisdom. The heart looks right past things that may offend our personal taste, often rejoicing in another's being, despite all our reasonable intentions to maintain a safe distance, play it cool, or break off contact if a relationship has become too painful. Love in its deepest essence knows nothing of conditions and is quite unreasonable. Once we allow our heart to open, we can become deeply touched by that person for the rest of our lives. Love is essentially an act of will. Spiritually evolved love is a decision to commit my life, above all else, to healing one other person, while stretching to expand my own lost parts."—John Welwood

"Love is the strand of sense that runs through our lives. It is the glue that keeps our fragmented lives together and purposeful."—Beverly Hutchinson, editor of A Course in Miracles Newsletter, The Holy Encounter

"Everything is relevant. I call it loving."—James Tate

"Love is an act of endless forgiveness, a tender look which becomes a habit!"—Peter Ustinov

"With love, even the rocks will open."
—Hazrat Inayat Khan

"The minute I heard my first Love Story, I started looking for you, not knowing how blind that was. Lovers don't finally meet somewhere, they're in each other all along."—Rumi

"Would you not go through fear to love? For such the journey seems to be." [2]—A Course in Miracles

WE WON'T TELL YOU

Along our walks to—we won't tell you
I say, "Listen—hear the surf."
As we come to the opening of our path
you say, "The waves are high.
Shall we go to Keawakapu instead?"
Then we see we are alone.
No intruders on our beach.
Just us—to read poems.
I'll call you the hundred pet names
that belong to only you.
You might even sing a love song
just for me.
Lets stay.
Take my hand through the surf.

— Natalie Tyler

—Notes—

–Notes–

2

The Difference Between Codependent Addiction and Lasting Deep Love

"I do not like you, but I love you.
Seems that I am always thinking of you.
Though you treat me badly, I love you madly.
You really got a hold on me."
—Smokey Robinson—

"Immature love says, 'I love you because I need you'. Mature love says, 'I need you because I love you'."
—Erich Fromm

I present to you, dear seeker, some definitions of the terms "codependency" and "addiction":

Codependency is a term used to describe an exaggerated dependent pattern of learned behaviors, beliefs and feelings that make life painful. It is a dependence on people and things outside the self, along with neglect of the self to the point of having little self-identity. Codependency is a specific condition that is characterized by preoccupation and extreme dependence—emotionally, socially and sometimes physically—on a person or object. Eventually, this dependency on another person becomes a pathological condition that affects the codependent in all other relationships.

Addiction is anything we feel tempted to lie about, anything we are not willing to give up, anything that keeps us unaware of what is going on inside us, that dulls and distorts our sensory input.

Brenda Schaeffer says, "Compulsive needing to possess another person is addictive love. Promoting the welfare of another is healthy love, and the soul's reaching out is spiritual soulful love."

ADDICTIONS ARE

- A compulsive need for something habit forming
- Repetition in action
- Destructive self hypnosis
- Non-growth—a way of being stuck in the past
- Blocked creative energy
- A masking of a real need
- Robotic reaction to life
- A false belief that something outside oneself can be a substitute for looking within
- Predictable, mechanistic, unconscious acts programmed from habit, founded on a stress reaction that happened in the past
- Replacement for God
- Our teacher—enough pain to finally get to the truth
- Distraction from our important purpose in life
- Inability to bond with at least one other person

Addiction = postponement
Addiction = attachment = Non Growth

We can recognize addiction by its lack of life giving qualities. It drains us of our Prime Energy—the energy to create. Love is the emotional oxygen that keeps humanity alive and the fuel that gives us energy to live. It is much broader than sexual attraction. Passionate, healthy love is exciting and peaceful, filled with tenderness, affection, sensuality, sexuality, appreciation, gratitude, comfort, communication, altruism and shared

THE DIFFERENCE BETWEEN CODEPENDENT ADDICTION & LASTING DEEP LOVE

dreams. The partners are able to count on each other in times of need. They give and receive emotional support. They mutually promote each other's welfare, and they enjoy each other's company.

Addictive codependency, often mistaken for love, is wildly emotional and confusing—a combination of passionate sexuality, pain, anxiety, relief, jealousy, elated drug-like highs, desperate lows, insecurity, and extremes of happiness and misery. The most obvious difference between healthy love and addictive codependency is that in healthy love there is passion and safety, while in addiction there is also passion, but a *lack* of safety.

© "Maxine," Marian Henley, Reprinted with Permission

Insecure people often use relationships to bolster their self-esteem and give themselves an identity and a direction. When one relationship ends, they search desperately for another. Relationship becomes a substitute for self-respect, and a reason to live. The addiction is like cotton candy—delicious for a short time, but nutritionally empty. Addictive codependency is similar to other addictions. The person needs more and more to feel satisfied, thinks about the next fix most of the time, prioritizes the relationship above all else, including safety, self-love and respect, peace and happiness. It is an unbalanced relationship, characterized both by excess emotion and lack of love. An overabundance of obsessive attention is bestowed on the other while an inadequate amount is given to the self, eventually to the point of self-abandonment.

Addictive love is like the July 4th fireworks display in the sky: all color and smoke and noise, and then it is over. Healthy love is sunrise and sunset every day, even with the passing clouds, and some days it is even more beautiful than the other days. You always know there is more, so a few clouds do not matter. It is a quiet, deep, satisfying fulfillment of passion, safety, bliss and ecstasy.

Addicts fall in love and it is a downward spiral, whereas lovers are friends who grow deeply in love and rise to a state of bliss. The biggest difference between rising and falling is the safety factor.

In addictive relationships we believe "I can't live without him!" We use the addictive relationship to blind ourselves to the intolerable reality of the other person or of our life. Remaining in an addictive relationship is harmful to our self-esteem, because it reinforces the notion that we are not worthy enough to deserve intimacy or commitment from a partner. We need to make friends with and nurture the child within us we left behind, and say "good-bye" to addiction and "hello" to self love. We need to love ourselves in order to love another and be loved in a healthy way. The trouble so many of us face is not the fact that we have not been loved, but that *we* have not learned to love. We have learned to take care of others instead of taking care of our own needs. We are in the Karpman Drama Triangle.*

The Drama Triangle consists of at least two people in an unequal relationship. There is always a Victim and either a Rescuer or Persecutor. Sometimes people switch

* Devised by Transactional Analyst Dr. Steve Karpman

THE DIFFERENCE BETWEEN CODEPENDENT ADDICTION & LASTING DEEP LOVE

roles. A person who rescues his victim parent frequently grows up unconsciously looking for a victim to rescue.

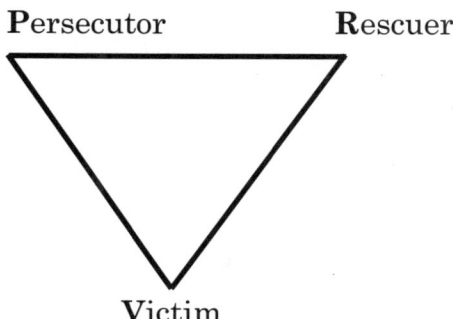

A Rescuer is someone who, on a regular basis, does any of the following:
- Does something for someone the other did not ask him to do.
- Does something for someone the other could do for himself.
- Does something for someone he resents doing.

A Persecutor blames others instead of looking within, criticizes, judges, and can be abusive verbally or physically. A Persecutor unconsciously attracts a Victim. A victim feels sorry for himself, stays stuck in the past, and maintains relationships with Rescuers or Persecutors who will enable him to continue being the Victim.

FROM CODEPENDENCY TO PARTNERSHIP

Codependency is an unequal relationship, usually between a Victim and a Rescuer or a Persecutor. A healthy, equal relationship only exists between whole partners who feel complete alone. Codependency stems from unhealthy childhood beginnings.

© Peter Mueller,
Reprinted with Permission

Some of the causes are:
• Low self esteem.
• Unresolved dependency with a parent.
• Blocked or punished natural attempts to separate emotionally from a parent, sometimes in the first few years, sometimes in adolescence.
• Lack of early bonding with a parent.
• Early loss or abandonment by a parent (death, divorce, adoption).
• Strong criticism or neglect by a parent.
• Being in a role reversal with a parent who is a Victim, so you take over as Rescuer.

Passivity results from codependency. Codependency interferes with autonomy, survival and gratification.

THE DIFFERENCE BETWEEN CODEPENDENT ADDICTION & LASTING DEEP LOVE

Codependents need the other person to be there because they have no sense of self; they are not fully in touch with themselves. They think that to be separate is dangerous. When they are alone and when their partner doesn't always meet all their needs, they fear abandonment; it reminds them of when they were little and the feeling of isolation was life-threatening.

In codependent relationships, decision making and options are limited, efficiency and problem solving are restricted. The more the relationship seems threatened, the more rigid it becomes. The relationship can become draining, as one or both partners feel weakened, as if they are losing a part of themselves. Frequently one partner feels invaded and has a fear of being engulfed, and tries to pull away; the other, feeling abandoned, becomes more clinging and sometimes hysterical, reinforcing the first partner's fears of engulfment.

In extreme cases, codependent people think they only exist "in merger", but they cannot tolerate the loss of self which results from being merged with another, so the belief is "I cannot exist." If the partner isn't available, they must desperately "connect" with a friend to believe in their own existence.

Codependents need to learn in therapy to:
• Increase self-expression of feelings in a straight, clear way, and also learn to control their self expression and avoid hysteria.
• Decrease guilt.
• Decrease fear of hurting others or succeeding "at other's expense," and understand their own hurt feelings derive from their childhood, not their partner's actions or lack of actions.
• Discover personal power and learn to enjoy it.
• Reduce fear of abandonment or engulfment.
• Work through grief at letting go of adapted self so real self can emerge.
• Recall and understand family patterns that led to

codependent beliefs and behaviors.
- Do inner child work, making redecisions from a child place talking to the parents of the past.
- Learn non-manipulative communication skills.
- Work through and let go of blaming others (including therapists) for problems or feelings. Take responsibility for everything they make happen.
- Work through transference and codependency with a therapist to form a healthy therapeutic partnership. Then take their parent's face off their partner and depend on themselves.

© Nicole Hollander, Reprinted with Permmission

We all have many parts to our personality. Transactional Analysis separates these into Parent, Adult and Child. The Parent is that part that has opinions and beliefs about right and wrong, values about what's good and bad, and expectations of self and others. The Parent

THE DIFFERENCE BETWEEN CODEPENDENT ADDICTION & LASTING DEEP LOVE

feels and behaves in the same way our parents, or whoever raised us, did. The Parent can be supportive and nurturing, or critical and controlling. The Critical Parent uses words like "You should" and points a finger.

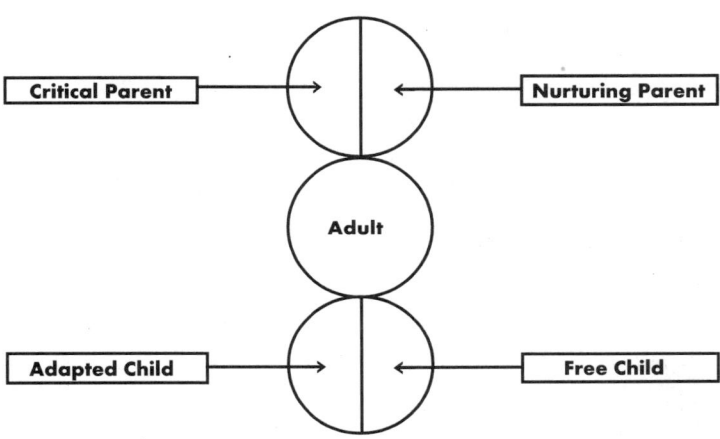

The Adult is that part that reasons things out, gathers information, draws conclusions from facts, and deals with reality. The Child is the part that has feelings, fantasies, wants and needs. The Child can be natural and free, or fearful and adaptive. The Adapted Child is either Compliant, taking care of and rescuing others, or Rebellious, resisting and angry. The Free Child says things like "I want", "I wish", "WOW!", "Oh, boy!" The Compliant Adapted Child says "That's OK" when it isn't, or "Whatever you want is OK." The Rebellious Adapted Child says "I want what I want now!" or "I don't care!" or "You can't make me!"

Sometimes control, neglect or abandonment in childhood sets up love addiction. The codependent does not know that she has enough power to take care of herself or that she can be with someone who can take care of himself. Sometimes she takes the Child role and makes the other person her parent who takes care of her, or she becomes the Parent and makes the other her child whom she takes care of. She becomes dependent on the other person and the relationship for her survival, and puts out unrealistic expectations. She wants the other person to make her OK, because she does not know she is already OK. She creates a fantasy about who the other person is and the fantasy wears off like a drunk wears off.

The addiction is a survival response often formed in childhood to provide comfort and relief from pain and internalized oppression. In an addictive personality there is a deficiency in the Nurturing Parent, Adult, or Free Child part of ourselves.

CODEPENDENT RELATIONSHIP BETWEEN TWO PEOPLE

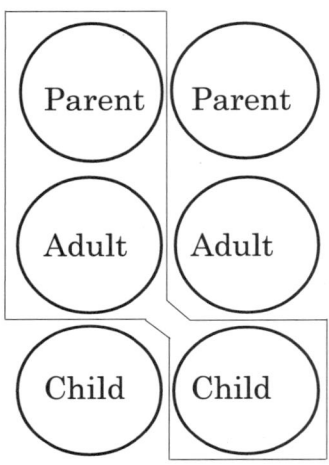

We thought we were making ourselves safe by either controlling the relationship or being controlled by the relationship. To make ourselves safe by controlling our relationship does not work. Controlling our feelings works. Addictive love or infatuation usually is filled with wild swings between jealousy over our insecurities about our partner, and relief when we find our fears are imaginary. It is characterized by wanting to become one with the lover. There is often anxiety about being loved in return, and the addict never feels loved enough and sometimes idealizes the lover and sometimes hates the lover. These desperate lovers fall in love easily and quickly with their own creation and fantasize and daydream easily. They are very sensitive to good-byes and separations and become defensive when criticized. Some do not show anger openly or directly, and others can be rageaholics.

THE DIFFERENCE BETWEEN CODEPENDENT ADDICTION & LASTING DEEP LOVE

Codependent love addicts are not likely to find lasting love without professional therapy.

As defined by Erich Fromm, love is "the expression of productiveness and implies care, respect, responsibility and knowledge; a striving towards growth and happiness of the loved person, rooted in one's own capacity to love."

Stanton Peale, author of *Love and Addiction*, defines addiction as "an unstable state of being, marked by a compulsion to deny all that you are or have been in favor of some new and ecstatic experience. It's a malignant outgrowth of normal human inclinations." Words associated with addiction are: excessive, obsessive, destructive, compulsive, habitual and dependency.

Love addiction is a reliance on someone external to self in an attempt to get unmet needs fulfilled, avoid fear, solve problems and maintain balance. The psychological reasons for love addiction are unique to each client. Finding out how love addiction makes sense to the individual is the task of therapy.

The purpose of a healthy relationship is mutual growth, fulfillment, the healing of wounds, fun, companionship, and someone to protect and respect our alone time and creative endeavors. The purpose of addictive relationships is to use the other person to assure ourselves of our existence. Codependent persons usually lack personal boundaries, and don't know where they end and the other begins. They are either compliant and put up with anything to "keep" their lover, or they hysterically demand more and more and more until they finally beat the other one down into submission or push him away.

"The power of love is the basis of the spiritual lover. The love of power is the basis of the addictive lover."
—Brenda Schaeffer

© Mark Stivers, Reprinted with Permission

—Notes—

—Notes—

3
Stages of Relationship

"The first step shall be to lose the way."
—Galway Kinnell

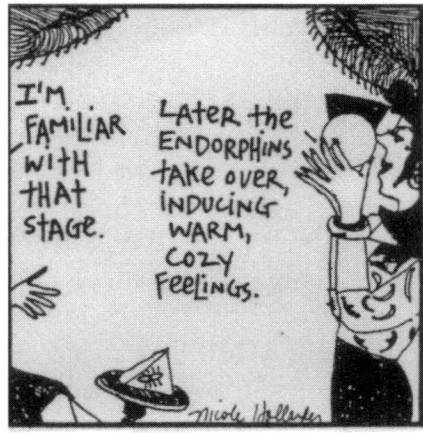

© Nicole Hollander, Reprinted with Permission

STAGES OF RELATIONSHIP

>Interesting drama:
>First act—Romance
>Second act—Power Struggle
>Third act is Love.
>Don't leave before the last act.
>Will you travel to another theater
>For the first two acts,
>Then leave again?
>—Natalie Tyler

"Seldom or never does a marriage develop into an individual relationship smoothly and without crisis. There is no birth of consciousness without pain." —C. G. Jung

NECESSARY, PREDICTABLE STAGES IN ALL RELATIONSHIPS*

All relationships go through predictable, necessary stages of development.

1. ROMANTIC — FUN — HONEYMOON — PSYCHOTIC ILLUSION STAGE

The first stage is the Romantic Stage, the delusional, honeymoon stage, when we "fall" in love and idealize the other person. We say "He's perfect for me," and we believe he is perfect. Of course we are both on our best behavior and only "showing" each other our best traits. We are not in reality enough to remind ourselves that no one is perfect.

Romance is Nature's anesthesia to blind you to your

---

*Adapted from *Getting the Love You Want*, by Harville Hendrix, with original changes and additions by the author.

STAGES OF RELATIONSHIP

partner's negative traits so emotional bonding can occur. It provides the glue that initially bonds two incomplete people together so they can begin the work of healing their childhood wounds.

2. POWER STRUGGLE STAGE

Then we find out this person is not perfect after all, and we feel crushed and disillusioned. We become needy, and we make ourselves feel mad, or sad, or scared, and our lover discovers some of our less flattering qualities as we desperately try to get that other "perfect" person back. As we learn about each other's character defects, we shift from the Romantic Stage into the Power Struggle Stage.

The purpose of this tense, conflict-filled second stage is to individuate and to get needs met in this relationship that were frustrated in childhood.

Unhappily, some couples stay in this stage for life, bickering, fighting, or becoming withdrawn from each other and just "sticking it out" in a life of unhappy resignation. People who are afraid of spiritual growth often go from one relationship to another and never stay through to get their lessons.

Fortunately, some couples do IMAGO Therapy (created by Harville Hendrix, Ph.D., author of Getting the Love You Want), or PAIRS® (Practical Application of Intimate Relationship Skills), or other work of professional marriage counselors. They learn to work through their differences and accept their challenges as important lessons they need to learn for their own spiritual growth. They courageously do the work to move to the next stage.

3. LEARNING, GROWING, TRANSFORMING STAGE

The next stage is the Path of Learning and Transformation. In this stage, couples make the transition from an unconscious to a conscious relationship.

Each looks within, takes responsibility for learning more about himself, his partner and the relationship. They stretch to heal each other's wounds and find the lost parts of themselves. They forgive and make closure with the past. They close all exits from the relationship and make a commitment to stay together no matter what.

Oh, for partners who have the courage and perseverance to stay in the relationship through these natural stages! The gift can be blissful, deep, enduring love in a safe, passionate, soul connected, committed partnership.

4. CONSCIOUS DEEP, SAFE PROFOUND FOREVER LOVE

In this final stage, the couple experiences deep, committed love and friendship, with feelings of passion, safety & equality—so much deeper than Romance. They have daily, open, honest communication, caring behaviors, fun, and conscious loving and sacred sex.

My husband and I have worked through the stages and have transformed our relationship into a love I did not know existed. We can't even remember what in the world we disagreed about in the Power Struggle Stage!

THE ROMANTIC STAGE

First comes the Romantic Stage, the honeymoon, that seemingly psychotic stage when we idealize this perfect person who can do no wrong. Frank Pittman, M.D. says, "I see Romantic love as an absurd, albeit delicious crisis-induced escape from sanity."

This beginning stage is Nature's way of drawing two people together in order to heal their childhood wounds. The wounds don't heal in this stage, but this strong attraction is necessary to bond these two people so they can go down this roller coaster relationship path together. Harville Hendrix' IMAGO theory sees Romantic Love as the way two people find each other who, during

STAGES OF RELATIONSHIP

their individual development, have been emotionally wounded in the same place. It is nature's way of helping us recreate that scene of our childhood in which the wounding occurred, so that we can at last get what we really needed back then.

Dr. Hendrix likes to call Romantic Love "Nature's anesthesia," because nature somehow numbs us to the faults of the person with whom we establish a love relationship so we will fall in love and create a strong emotional bond which will sustain us through the next stages of the relationship. And nature does this in order to fulfill its purpose: to heal the wounds of our childhood and provide us with what we need to finish our development—so we can grow!

Romantic love is not love, but a complex of attitudes *about* love. Love does not suffer by being freed from the belief system of romantic love. Love improves and reaches heretofore unknown heights when it is distinguished from romance. When the romantic spell is broken, you have the opportunity to see that the person you love and the projection you've pasted over him are separate realities. Now you have the *power* to see him as he is, to relate to him as a real person and value him as a person, rather than as the carrier of your lost soul and your unlived life.

When you stop pretending your lover is the idealized being of your fantasies, you can know him as an equal individual, as he really is, and you can relate to the beauty hidden until now. Breaking the romantic spell provides a golden opportunity to discover the real person who is there, and instead of living through him, you can take responsibility for living your own unlived life. The Romantic Stage begins with falling "in love", which happens in the lower self. During the fourth stage of relationship, our Higher Selves "rise" in love.

Robert A. Johnson says: "People never settle into relationships with each other as flesh and blood human beings, until they are out of the romantic love stage and love each other instead of being 'in love' with a fantasy. Romantic love fools us. It looks as if it aims at making a real relationship out of what we pretend. Oh. The vast difference!—between relating to a human person and using that person as a vehicle for one's projection."

The cult of romance teaches us that ordinary people are not enough. In the romantic stage, we try hard to pretend what our partner has idealized. He has made us up from scratch, but we're genetically wired to be who we really are, and we feel uncomfortable pretending to be someone different. Stress comes from trying to be someone we're not. We often feel like we're not loved enough, and there's a hole in our heart, because who we really are is not known and loved.

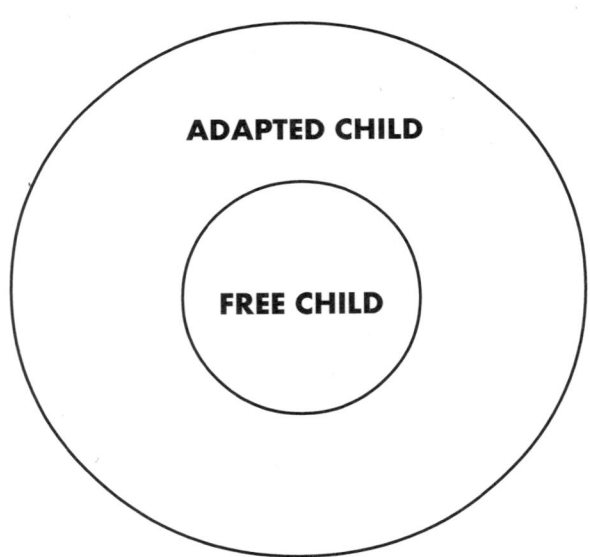

In the Romantic Stage we are adapting to our partner's idealized vision of who we are; we're not being our true self. Our Adapted Child part is hiding our Free Child —our heart center—who cannot come out to play. And the Free Child is the one who connects emotionally with another. All intimacy comes from Free Child to Free Child. The Adapted Child only pays attention to others and tries to do what will please them, and the real self gets lost in the relationship.* True intimacy can only exist when two people are each being themselves.

During this first stage of the relationship, the two lovers are focused on maintaining their intense closeness. They stare into each other's eyes for hours, dance the night away, and experience skyrocketing sex. This is Nature's way of bringing them together with enough electrifying attachment to do the real work of healing and growth that is yet to come.

THE POWER STRUGGLE STAGE

Sam Keen says, "The conflict in marriage is the forge of the spirit." And John Wellwood says, "The characteristics in your partner you most dislike —that's grist for the mill of your soul work."

Reprinted with Permission
"The Born Loser," Newspaper Enterprise Association

After we've been in the Romantic Stage for a while we both "get real". We begin to notice our partner has changed. We start to see problems, negative traits and habits (everyone has them!), and preferences different from our own. "Opposites" fall in love. The Clinger falls in love with the Avoider. The Isolater falls for the Fuser.

*Adapted Child and Free Child are explained in Chapter 2.

The Rigid personality finds the Diffuser, and the Competitive person looks for the Passive/Manipulator. And the Longer (Victim) finds the Caretaker (Rescuer)—often the alcoholic/dependent couple. Nature, as IMAGO theory defines it, determines that two people *injured at the same place developmentally* find each other and fall in love! We each want our own way, and we hate facing the lack of perfection in the other. We feel shocked and angry, and lo and behold, we are now in the Power Struggle Stage! We fight and keep fighting; or we become indifferent and withdraw emotionally while staying in a relationship of boredom or affairs; or we separate (perhaps divorce); or we S-T-R-E-T-C-H and grow to learn to accept the "imperfections". Sometimes this takes some sessions with a marriage counselor or psychotherapist, or Harville Hendrix' IMAGO Therapy. In our Happily Married Forever program we help people heal their wounds and have better relationships than they ever imagined. Your partner has the blueprint for your growth! Brenda Schaeffer says, "Problems in relationships cannot always be resolved. They must be outgrown and transcended. This is what spiritual lovers do."

"The work being done on your marriage—are you having it done, or are you doing it yourselves?"

Reprinted with Permission © The New Yorker Collection, 1989 Michael Maslin from cartoonbank.com, All Rights Reserved

As we enter the Power Struggle Stage, we are beginning to realize how different our styles are, how many areas of disagreement there are between us. One or both feels the need for more time apart. At least one starts thinking "Can I be myself in this relationship?" We think we need walls of protection, so we construct them. We sometimes feel confused about whether to stay in the relationship or not. Confusion is a very high space. It comes just before enlightenment. We try power plays as a misguided way to ease our confusion. Anais Nin says, "It is not failed relationships which influence our life — they influence our death."

POWER PLAYS

A power play is a transaction in which one person obtains from another person something that he wants against the other person's will. The power play may involve physical force or mental or psychological pressure and manipulation. In a primary relationship power plays are typically used to get our partner to conform to our desires and beliefs.

Power plays often involve attempts to get our partner to feel guilty or ashamed. Guilt and shame are not true feelings. They consist of two parts: first, there is a self-judgment that "I did something wrong"; this is followed by a bad feeling —scared, angry (at myself as well as others), or sad. Reject the judgment and you will avoid the nasty feelings of shame and guilt. Despair is also a judgment—that the situation is hopeless or that I am helpless. Restore hope or find a way to resolve the situation and the bad feelings can be prevented or eliminated. We need to look for options, alternatives, new ways of thinking and doing that respect each other's equality and autonomy.

Reprinted with Permission, Mister Boffo © Joe Martin, Distributed by Universal Press Syndicate, All Rights Reserved

CHARACTERISTICS OF POWER PLAYS

The transition from childish omnipotence to power sharing seems to be something we all struggle with in childhood, through adolescence, and on into our adult life. Confusion over the uses of power is evident in unhealthy, uneasy adult relationships. Here are some of the power plays that sabotage adult lover relationships:
• Giving advice but not accepting it.
• Having difficulty reaching out and asking for support and love.
• Giving orders; demanding and expecting much from others.
• Trying to "get even" or to diminish the self esteem or power of others.
• Being judgmental; put downs that sabotage others' successes; faultfinding; persecuting; punishing.
• Holding out on others; not giving what others want or need.
• Making, then breaking promises; causing others to trust us and then betraying the trust.
• Smothering; over-nurturing the other.
• Patronizing, condescending treatment of the other that sets one partner up as superior and the other as inferior; intimidation.
• Making decisions for the other; discounting the other's

STAGES OF RELATIONSHIP

ability to solve problems.
- Putting the other in no-win situations.
- Attempting to change the other (and unwillingness to change oneself).
- Attacking the other when he or she is most vulnerable.
- Showing an anti-dependent attitude: "I don't need you."
- Using bullying, bribing behavior; using threats.
- Showing bitterness, self-righteous anger, or holding grudges.
- Abusing others verbally, physically or emotionally.
- Being aggressive and defining it as assertiveness.
- Needing to win or be right.
- Resisting stubbornly or being set in one's own way.
- Having difficulty admitting mistakes or saying "I'm sorry."
- Giving indirect, evasive answers to questions.
- Defending any of the behaviors on this list.

What does power have to do with marriage? Everything! Without power we cannot exist, and to be in a partnership, we must be able to be separate. The Power Struggle stage is a stage of individuating, a repeat of the stage we went through as children when we had to individuate from our parents in order to know who we were. Now we need to know who we are in our love relationship. John Bosenthal says in *Insisting on Love*, "We are not rocks. Who wants to be one anyway, impermeable, unchanging, our history already played out."

So for a while we get lost in our differences—if you don't get lost, there's a chance you may never be found. This is the time when some people resist, because resistance is natural right before change takes place. Those who are afraid of change and don't have the stamina for the struggle break up or divorce during the Power Struggle Stage, instead of working it through to love. There's a Senegalese proverb that says "Three kinds of people die poor: those who divorce; those who incur debts; and those who move around too much." Some people keep leaving relationships at the Power Struggle Stage, and then they go on to the next romance, and never stay long enough to get their lessons and grow into love.

In easy relationships where no one ever disagrees or argues, we don't learn much and we may stay stuck in the past. In more difficult relationships where we acknowledge each other's differences and embrace each other's differences, there are great opportunities for growth and spiritual development. When we use relationships only for comfort and security, they stagnate, putting us more deeply asleep and reinforcing habitual patterns of fear and self-doubt.

Frustrations in relationships are a little bit about now and a lot about the house you each grew up in. To get to the spiritual level attainable in marriage, each of you must go through the developmental stages you are stuck in from childhood. In IMAGO therapy you develop the empathy necessary to heal your developmental wounds. IMAGO Relationship Theory sees marriage as nature's way of giving individuals a second chance to have their developmental needs noticed, practiced and mastered.

If you don't stay and complete the task in each stage, you may have to come back and do it later with someone else. In the evolution of consciousness, our greatest problem is often our greatest opportunity. Usually what your partner, who knows you so well, wants you to do differently is exactly what you need to do for your own awakening and growth. I invite you to seize the opportunity!

Some other helpful hints for couples in a Power Struggle:
• When you feel stuck and do not know how to proceed, go back into your memory and remember family interactions. The key is there. This is not to blame parents. More importantly, this is an opportunity to discover *how* family interactions influenced the behavior manifested in

STAGES OF RELATIONSHIP 63

your present relationship.
- Marital struggles are unfinished business with parents or battles observed between parents. In the family, patterns of behavior are learned as ways of coping with stresses. In marriage, scenes from the family are re-enacted over and over in an effort to resolve or complete what was left unfinished from childhood.
- Projection is the mechanism by which we see in our partner the unacceptable behaviors that were experienced in our family of origin.
- The process of separating the present problem from the original wound takes time, patience and tender loving care both for yourself and your partner.
- It is crucial in dealing with power struggles that you stay focused on and connected to your partner in the present and rediscover that person whenever you lose touch with him.
- Respond to each other's pain with empathy and understanding and nurture each other in the relationship. This is vital for the growth of intimacy between you.

Zen Buddhism teaches that inner growth always involves an experience of a red hot coal stuck in the throat. We can't swallow it, and we can't cough it up. This hot coal alerts us that a tremendous evolutionary potential is trying to manifest itself. This is your opportunity to stretch, find the lost parts of yourself that your partner is calling upon you to demonstrate, embark on the inner quest and take on the divine work of becoming whole! David Carradine says, "There's an alternative. There's always a third way, and it's not a combination of the other two ways. It's a different way."

Reprinted with Permission, Mister Boffo © Joe Martin, Distributed by Universal Press Syndicate, All Rights Reserved

LEARNING AND TRANSFORMATION

"I have woven a parachute out of everything broken."
—William Stafford

"A good relationship is based on mutual respect and a relatively equal balance of power. It involves concern for and sensitivity to each other's feelings and needs, as well as an appreciation of the things that make each partner so special. . . Within this idea, there is room for arguments, bad moods, differences of opinions, even anger. However, loving partners find effective ways of dealing with their differences. They do not view each other as a battle to be won or lost." —Susan Forward

The secret to moving from the Power Struggle Stage into the Learning and Transforming Stage is to shift from a protective, closed position into an open and non-defensive place. In times of stress all our childhood instincts cry out for protection, protection for the powerless child, and our automatic response is to shut down and become defensive. Our intent is to protect ourselves at all costs. Mired in our fear, we take one of three positions:
• We attempt to control the situation by threats or intimidation;
• We give in to our partner's demands to avoid their anger

STAGES OF RELATIONSHIP

and disapproval; or
• We pretend to be indifferent, and we withdraw or shut down.

These are the coping skills most of us learned as children, and they do not work in our adult relationships. As the great German poet, Werner Maria Rilke, says, "The only way to move through the disappointment of relationships without harming yourself and others is to open your heart more at the very moment you most want to close it off." To open your heart when you feel so threatened is an act of conscious intention, and requires great courage. When you open your heart in this way, you learn about yourself, your childhood wounds, your partner and her childhood wounds, and your relationship. With this conscious shift, you take control of your response. You come from a position of great personal power, unlike your childhood when you had no real power to protect yourself.

This shift in consciousness allows you to see the present as it really is: not life threatening. You are not under attack by your enemy; this is your partner, the one you love who is in pain. You can learn to hear the difference. You cannot protect yourself and be open to learning at the same time.

When you develop this ability to remain open during conflict, you are able to see your partner in a new way: as someone who is wounded and in pain. This new way of seeing your partner enables you to respond to her needs with empathy and compassion, to stretch to meet her needs, rather than reacting with fear of being controlled or "told what to do". This new understanding of your partner and yourself lifts your relationship to a new level of caring and connection, the beginning of transformation and true intimacy.

Lasting intimacy is impossible without the feeling that each partner is equally important and equally valu-

able. Some of the ways to achieve the balance of power are:
• Expand the boundaries of the relationship so each partner will bring forth their hidden aspects into full view.
• Reconcile differences by accepting "negative" traits or unfamiliar views and releasing rigidities.
• Share your wounds with each other and commit to a mutual healing.
• Get help from an IMAGO therapist, a PAIRS® Master therapist, or other psychotherapist who specializes in couples therapy. Just as you would go to a dentist for a tooth ache, a chiropractor for a back ache, or a medical doctor or naturopath for other physical ailments, so it is quite practical to go together to a specialist who heals the wounds of the heart.

"Contact is the appreciation of differences."
—Fritz Perls
"...and the recognition of similarities."
—Richard Price

You can work through the Power Struggle Stage by learning that the true test of spirituality is being able to be happy with someone who is different. Deal with who you and your partner really are—that's when love becomes fun.

In the Power Struggle Stage, all our buttons get pushed. If we look closely, we'll recognize that we've unconsciously chosen a partner with some of the same negative traits of one or both of our parents. This is a great opportunity to heal our childhood wounds if we will stay and make the unconscious conscious. We can work through the Power Struggle Stage to the other side if we stretch to heal each other's childhood wounds. One of the best ways to learn to stretch is to engage in the Parent/Child Dialogue exercise developed by Harville Hendrix.

STAGES OF RELATIONSHIP

PARENT/CHILD DIALOGUE

Select a time and place where you will not be disturbed for at least an hour.

Decide who will be the SENDER and who will be the RECEIVER.

The person who chooses to be the SENDER takes the "child" role. The RECEIVER sits in a comfortable position and holds the SENDER as a mother would hold a baby at her breast. The RECEIVER plays the role of first one parent, then the other, while the SENDER talks "as a child" to each parent.

The RECEIVER, in the role of the "as if" parent, prompts the SENDER as follows:
RECEIVER: "I am your mother/father. What is it like living with me?"
SENDER: [describes hurts and pains in childhood with this/these parents.]
RECEIVER: "If I got it right, living with me is..." [mirrors only what Sender has said]
Then asks: "Is there more about that?"
SENDER: Continues to talk about childhood hurts until there is "no more".
RECEIVER: Continues to mirror and ask "is there more?" until Sender indicates there is no more.
[When SENDER says there is "no more," RECEIVER continues.]
RECEIVER: "What is your worst frustration and deepest hurt with me?"
SENDER: "My worst frustration and deepest hurt with you is..." [describes the frustration and hurt].
RECEIVER: [Mirrors] "If I got it right, your worst frustration and deepest hurt with me is...Is there more?" [Continues to mirror and ask for more until Sender indicates there is "no more".]
RECEIVER: "As your mother/father, what do you need

from me the most that would heal all that?"
SENDER: "What I need most from you is..." [describes the deepest need]
RECEIVER: [Mirrors] "If I got it right, what you need the most from me, as your mother/father, is...Is there more about that?"
SENDER: [continues until all is said about that]
RECEIVER: [Mirrors until there is no more, then says] "I want you to have all that. As your partner, what can I do now that would heal all that with your mother/father?"
SENDER: "What I need most from you now to heal all that with my mother/father is..." [describes a specific behavior desired from the partner related to the wound with the parent].
RECEIVER: [Mirrors] "If I got it right, what you need most from me now that would heal all that with your mother/father is...Is there more about that?" until Sender is through.
RECEIVER: "As your partner, I want to give that to you, and I will grow into it." [Continue to hold "child" for a few moments to allow the child to experience getting his needs met, and to savor the closeness.] Then repeat exercise, with RECEIVER as other parent.

When RECEIVER has played role of both parents, switch roles and repeat entire exercise.

The important part of this exercise is to stretch in the ways your partner asks you to stretch, even though it may be difficult. Stretching in this way is essential for your partner's healing and for your own growth—your partner always calls upon you to do the thing you most need to do to find the lost part of yourself—and for a happy relationship. Love is more important than being right. This is the surest way to graduate from the Power Struggle Stage into Learning and Transformation, which is the bridge to deep, lasting Conscious Love. Pain in our love life is an opportunity to spiritually transform ourselves so we can know a deeper level of love and personal power. Gerald G. Jampolsky, M.D. says, "All healing involves replacing fear with love."

FOREVER LOVE—THE FINAL STAGE—CONSCIOUS RELATIONSHIP

"Never mind. The self is the least of it. Let our scars fall in love." —Galway Kinnell

The essential ingredients for abiding love are affection, stability, loyalty, and commitment, not romance. Jungian analyst Robert A. Johnson says, "If we look clearly we see that romance is a completely different energy system, a completely distinct set of values from love and commitment. If it is romance we seek, it is romance we shall have (but not commitment and not relationship)."

After graduating from the Power Struggle Stage through Learning and Transformation, you have the task of learning to love yourself. You must love yourself, with all your frailties and mistakes, in order to love one other person fully. When you feel complete in yourself, you stop expecting your beloved to complete you.

Ah! Love at last! We still have differences and we've stretched, so the arguments aren't as often and they're over quickly. We now are able to put less importance on superficial differences, and we put love, healing, and happiness first. How good it feels!

"Love is a path toward far deeper experiences of the soul. The loss of will and control one feels in love is highly nutritious for the soul. Love keeps the soul on track of its fate and keeps consciousness at the edge of the abyss of infinity that is the range of the soul. There is no way toward divine love except through the discovery of human intimacy and community. One feeds the other."
— Thomas Moore

—Notes—

4

Conscious Marriage*

"Couples need to commit to the process of creating a new kind of relationship: *the conscious marriage.* The first step in transforming a relationship into a conscious marriage is in the realization of a simple truth: The unconscious purpose of marriage for people who fall in love is to help each other finish childhood. To get the love they want, partners in a relationship must bring this unconscious purpose into awareness, and mutually commit to giving each other the nurturing and validation they did not receive from their parents."
—Dr. Harville Hendrix—
Getting the Love You Want

"The purpose of marriage, or a committed, monogamous, intimate love relationship, is to force and foster the development of the undeveloped, originally projected aspects of both personalities."—Don Lathrop, M.D.

"No one is where he is by accident, and chance plays no part in God's plan."[1]—A Course in Miracles

"No snowflake ever falls in the wrong place."
— Zen saying

---

* I am indebted to Harville Hendrix, Ph.D. for his concept of Conscious Marriage, and for some of the diagrams and exercises in this Chapter.

HAPPILY MARRIED FOREVER

FOR BETTER OR FOR WORSE

© Lynn Johnston
Reprinted with Permission

MIRRORS
(To my soulmate wife, Natalie)

Breath of my breath
Skin of my skin
Vision of my vision
I love the you
beneath the you
beneath the you.
Heart of my heart
Soul of my soul
For my own good
I love you.
—John Tyler

In a conscious marriage couples have graduated from the Power Struggle Stage we explain in Chapter 3 into rich, deep love, and they commit to be together forever. The two most important ingredients in a conscious marriage are safety and passion. The safety comes from closing all exits and eliminating criticism and verbal and physical abuse. The most common exits are:
• Addictions (drugs, alcohol, TV, shopping, workaholism, Internet—anything done compulsively, taking energy out of the relationship).
• Affairs or flirting.
• Divorce.
• Threatening divorce.
• Going crazy, even temporarily through anger.
• Threatening suicide or dangerous behavior—driving recklessly, other dangerous pursuits.

An exit is any feeling you express behaviorally that avoids your partner and diminishes intimacy.

An exit is being used when there is conscious and/or unconscious avoidance of your partner.

In order for the energy to be used for growth, it must be reinvested in your partner by closing exits.

DIAGRAM: The Invisible Divorce

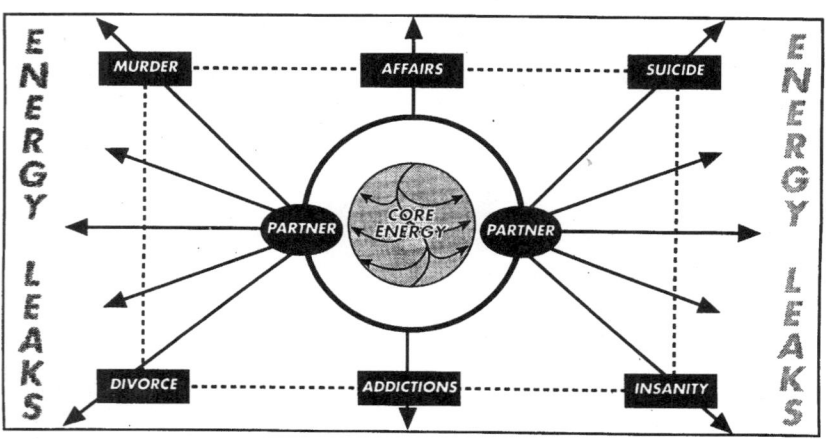

Instructions: Identify your exits and share them with your partner. Note these examples:
• I agree to keep you safe—No murder, abusive anger or drugs.
• I agree to stay in the relationship—No divorce or affairs.
• I agree to limit my TV viewing and spend an hour with you each evening.

There is a natural flow of cycles in a healthy relationship, times when one is a nurturing parent and the other a child, and then other times when it switches. We come more into balance by remembering we have a child within who needs nurturing as much as an inner parent who needs to nurture.

CONSCIOUS MARRIAGE

Conscious Marriage requires reclaiming the lost, repressed parts of ourselves, and learning more effective coping mechanisms than the crying, anger or withdrawal

CONSCIOUS MARRIAGE 75

which have become habitual for us. We must change to give our partner what he needs no matter how difficult it is, no matter how much it goes against the grain of our personality and temperament. We S-T-R-E-T-C-H to become the person our partner needs us to be to heal. We redesign our relationship to complete the unfinished business of our childhood. Our *unconscious* aim—to become whole, to restore our joyful aliveness—must become our *conscious* intention. Our goal is to become passionate friends with our partner, to develop "Reality Love" based on knowledge, care, respect and value of the other. Here are Harville Hendrix' *Guidelines for a Conscious Marriage* to which we have added many of our own original components and quotes from wise teachers:

• Tell each other our childhood wounds, and say what we need from each other to help heal those wounds and make us feel loved.

• Use that information to change our old patterns of behavior, so we see our partner as wounded, respond to him with empathy, and understand that his conflictual behavior arises out of his pain. Barry and Joyce Vissell, the doctor-nurse team who wrote *The Shared Heart*, say, "Many times the difficulty with your partner is the very thing compelling your development."

• Discover and discard inappropriate beliefs from childhood and call each other back to original wholeness. Replace our inappropriate behaviors and defensive strategies with openness, vulnerability and love.

• Keep each other physically and emotionally safe at all times, with no verbal or physical abuse.

• Close all escape hatches or exits from the relationship, and end all behaviors that avoid intimacy. "Safety is the complete relinquishment of attack."—A Course in Miracles[2].

• Communicate fully and openly every day.

• Bond daily, be physically affectionate, and have non-goal-oriented sex.

- Re-Romanticize your relationship by giving each other caring behaviors on a daily basis with no strings attached, including compliments, praise and appreciation. Another piece of wisdom from Barry and Joyce Vissell in *The Shared Heart*: "We each have a tremendous spiritual responsibility to those we love. By focusing on the beauty and greatness in one another, we can actually bring these qualities to the surface."
- Keep the spark alive by sharing high energy fun, laughter and romantic times daily, and surprises monthly.
- Eliminate criticism and blame. Express all needs as requests for behavior changes, and ask directly for what you want. Convert all frustrations into behavior change requests through the Daily Temperature Reading (Observations with Request for Change) and Fair Fight for Change. Express all anger and rage by appointment only, in the format of a Haircut or Vesuvius. (See Chapters 5 & 6 for these tools).
- S-T-R-E-T-C-H to give our partner what she wants and needs no matter how difficult that is. One last quote from love teachers Barry and Joyce Vissell from *The Shared Heart* (or maybe second from last!): "As long as our dreams and goals are more important to us than those of our partner, we prevent ourselves from experiencing Divine Love."
- Create a Relationship Vision of the relationship we would like to have.

Remember—by S-T-R-E-T-C-H-I-N-G to give our partner what he needs, we heal our own wounds. In giving our partner what is hardest for us to give, we reclaim our hidden selves, because stretching requires us to overcome our fears and defenses and move into being all of who we are. As we S-T-R-E-T-C-H to love our partner, our pain and self-absorption diminish, we begin to feel safe, and we are more available to meet our partner's needs. The barrier to love is self-hatred. When we break down our self-hatred by meeting our partner's needs and reclaiming our hidden selves, then we can truly love our partner. A Conscious Relationship is a spiritual path, which leads us home again to joy and aliveness, to the feeling of oneness we started out with.

A relationship not devoted to a higher purpose is bound to fail. What better higher purpose than to heal your beloved's wounds, find the lost part of yourself, and together practice loving kindness as role models for everyone with whom you come in contact? The love between two people contains the presence of God, and you will have a healing effect on everyone you meet.

Conscious marriages contain profound possibilities for healing. A conscious marriage is a sacred path that calls on us to cultivate the fullness and depth of who we are. In a conscious marriage we are aware of choosing this particular person because in the beginning, unconsciously in some ways, that person reminded us of one of our parents—usually the one who pushed our buttons—the one who left us with unfinished business or unhealed childhood wounds. All marriages are haunted by ghosts from the past. When we become aware of this reality and we share our deepest wounds with each other, we've started our adventure into healing. We then S-T-R-E-T-C-H to heal each other's wounds and in so doing find the lost parts of ourselves. Barry Kaufman of The Options Institute says, "To heal is to make happy."

I can best explain how partners in relationship stretch to heal each other's childhood wounds by telling you our own story. As a little toddler in Cincinnati on Chalfonte Avenue, my mother put me outside on a little rocking chair *all morning* with a doll and pink blanket, and told me to "sit there and be good." Receiving no attention or stimulation, I went inside myself and made up stories and developed a rich fantasy life, but I desperately craved attention. My sister 6 years older was in school. As I grew, my mother still did not seem interested in me—not my words, my school, my boy friends—not anything. By the time I was a young teenager who could have greatly benefited from a mother's interest, my sister was married and having babies, and my mother seemed obsessed with my sister's life, and even less interested in mine.

When my father wasn't working he was listening to the radio, doing crossword puzzles, and reading the newspaper, *Liberty Magazine*, and *The Saturday Evening Post*. He was distant and seemed afraid of me. By the time I married the man of my dreams, I was more desperate than ever for attention—to be heard.

We are unconsciously moved to marry our IMAGO—someone who has some of the negative traits of one or our parents, so I chose over and over men with short attention spans. With John I hit the jackpot. He has a long attention span. He loves to read and reads at every opportunity—several books a week. When he wanted to read instead of listen to me, that triggered my emotional allergy—not being heard, receiving no attention—causing me so much pain that I began criticizing him for reading so much, even though I had searched the world over for a man who reads as much as I do.

When I criticized him and tried to change him, it brought up his emotional allergy: being criticized by his father, who demanded perfection. As a child, when his father criticized him he would lose himself in books. So we were developing a system of reliving our childhood wounds: I wanted to be heard, so I demanded his attention and criticized him when I did not get it; when I criticized him, he withdrew and concentrated more and more on his reading. I became more demanding and critical, and what do you think happened next? He read more than ever!

Conscious awareness to the rescue!!! One day in "The Happy Valley" in Massachusetts, we went cross country skiing. Everything was pristine white, peaceful and still. The trees and the ground all through the woods were covered with new snow, and there wasn't a sound in the forest. At this hour we seemed to be the only humans anywhere. I fully took in the western Massachusetts enchantment of the moment. I looked into the eyes of my Snowman husband, and broke the sacred silence with, "I love you. Let's never criticize each other again, and let's always quietly listen to each other for as long as needed." He looked at me with his brown soul windows, and shouted "Yes!" which echoed back to us "Yes!" from the magic mountain. When we returned home, we lit a fire in the fireplace and drank a toast of hot buttered rum. We shared more fully than ever before feelings we had stored from our childhood wounds, and we each listened intently without interrupting and with open hearts and ears.

Then we made a mutual commitment to stretch to help each other heal those wounds: I agreed not to criticize him, and he agreed to stop whatever he was doing and listen to me for at least 10 minutes. This outcome has healed our childhood wounds and gifted us with the splendor of a conscious marriage. When I committed to stop being critical, I healed his emotional allergy, and at the same time I reclaimed the lost part of myself—the part who is loving, accepting and understanding. I was able to grow and use those same skills I stretched into with my clients, our children and our friends. When John agreed to put his book down and give me his full attention for as long as I needed it, he found the lost part of himself—the part who is attentive, aware and consciously interested in what others have to say. He enjoys his therapy practice, our children and friends more, now that he's not tuning out a part of what people say the way he learned in his childhood. The universe as usual brought two people together who could share their wounds, heal each other, integrate the lost parts of themselves, and develop a conscious marriage.

Whenever we forget, we remind each other to "close

your beautiful eyes and see the snow covering the landscape, and remember the mountains echoing 'Yes!'" Here in Hawaii surrounded by gentle green wherever we look, we remember, and life is good.

Your partner acts as a substitute for your parents—to help you re-experience the blocked pains of your childhood which live forever in your mind. If we had an angry parent in childhood, we'll pick an angry person for a partner because it's what we became accustomed to. If we were neglected or not given enough attention in childhood, we might choose a busy or withdrawn partner, thinking this time we'll make it turn out right. We might be so desperate to get our needs met that we mistakenly inflict pain to get pleasure, and it doesn't work. When we inflict pain, we get pain back instead. Partners need to help each other redo their childhoods and be the nurturing parent to each other that their parents may not have known how to be, or perhaps, because of their life circumstances, they didn't have the time for what you needed. Whatever our partner needs us to do to help heal her wounds is usually exactly what we need to change for our own growth—to find the lost part of ourselves and be all of who we can be.

You can do the Parent/Child Dialogue in Chapter 3. Then follow through by remembering your partner's wounds: instead of seeing him as difficult, angry, threatening, dangerous, or selfish, see him as wounded, and respond with empathy, and know that *all conflictual behavior arises out of pain.* You unconsciously chose him *for your own healing.* Harville Hendrix calls this the "IMAGO"—the image of a parent figure with whom you have hurts or unfinished business.

© Copyright Marian Henley, Reprinted with Permission

Barry & Joyce Vissell say in *The Shared Heart*: "Learning to love one other person completely teaches you how to love all people." A Course in Miracles says, "Everything is for your own best interests."[3] Marianne Williamson says: "Spiritual progress is like detoxification. Things have to come up in order to be released. Once we have asked to be healed, then our unhealed places are forced to the surface, as temples of healing. Relationships are like a trip to the Divine physician's office. How can a doctor help us unless we show him our wounds? The ego seeks to use a relationship to fill our needs as we define them."

In a conscious relationship the possibilities for growth are endless, and both partners transcend their pasts and rise to new levels of experience. In unconscious relationships, when people are angry, hurt, or fearful, they often put up a wall to protect themselves. Emerson said, "Every wall is a door." I say the door is *empathy*: "Honey, I'm sorry you're so upset (or angry, or distant, etc.). I love you. How can I help?" In some situations, "Can I hold you? Do you want to be comforted in my arms?" That's the door to love, healing, and happiness.

Our Higher Self asks that relationship be a way to support, heal, and bring joy to each other, all others, and to the planet.

RE-IMAGING

In a conscious relationship, you see your partner as wounded and respond to your partner with empathy, and all conflictual behavior is understood as arising out of pain. As a result of power struggles and old-fashioned dysfunctional ways of fighting, in which both partners said and did things which hurt the other person, we began to see our partner as threatening and a source of danger to us.

Re-imaging means changing from seeing your partner as threatening and dangerous to seeing your partner as wounded and in pain. From that perspective, when your partner is oversensitive or reacts in ways that frustrate you, you see your partner as frightened by your behavior and self-protective, rather than "bad," and you express understanding and empathy instead of being counter-reactive. Your relationship, then, can become a source of healing. Your most important achievement is to understand more clearly that your partner has a childhood wound and that you are wounded also.

As D.H. Lawrence says, "One must learn to love, and go through a good deal of suffering to get to it . . . and the journey is always toward the soul."

TRANSFORMATIONAL RELATIONSHIP AS THE SPIRITUAL PATH TO ENLIGHTENMENT AND BLISS

A. **Communication**

  1. Regular, honest, open, full sharing of thoughts and feelings.
  2. No secrets, no lies, no games. Mutual self-disclosure.
  3. Vast amounts of expressions of love, appreciation, and admiration toward each other daily.
  4. Both partners say 100% of what they want.

B. **Responsibility**

  1. Both partners take full responsibility for everything they make happen, and avoid blaming the other. They both stay open and are willing to learn about each other, instead of being closed and defensive to protect themselves.
  2. They take responsibility for their own interests and friends, and don't depend on the relationship to get all their needs met.

C. **Cooperation**

  1. No competition, power plays, or scorekeeping.
  2. Both people believe that a cooperative solution can be found to any differences.
  3. They have equal rights and responsibilities.
  4. All solutions are renegotiable at any time.
  5. No rescues. Avoid the Drama Triangle*
  6. Both accept demands and put up with shortcomings.

* The Karpman Drama Triangle is explained in Chapter 2.

D. Commitment

1. Each is the most important "other" in partner's life.
2. They agree to stay together forever and meet as many of partner's wants and needs as possible without compromising personal integrity or autonomy.
3. Commitment includes committing to:
   a. Staying alive and healthy
   b. Not withdrawing and staying withdrawn
   c. Not driving the other away
   d. Not being passive
4. Both persons are emotional support systems for each other.
5. Both agree there is no scarcity.
6. Relationship comes first, before anything else.

E. Physical

1. They express love sexually and are physically affectionate.
2. They create time to be alone together.
3. Lots of caring behaviors—large and small.
4. Bonding and transcendental lovemaking rather than just genital sex.

F. Spiritual

1. Both partners exercise the will to extend themselves for the purpose of nurturing their own and their partner's spiritual growth.
2. They seek an understanding and acceptance of their own and the other's life purpose.
3. Similar values.
4. Minimal talk about small issues and relationship processing from lower self.
5. Maximum higher self sharing about loving feelings, beautiful thoughts, planetary and social consciousness, new learnings, dreams, and goals.

CONSCIOUS MARRIAGE

You never really know
When you meet your Imago.
Is it an exchange of names
Or is it with the eyes?
That ask...Can you... Will you
Maybe... Love me?
Did we meet when we were
Only a dream of each other?
Or did we meet with
The cries of heal me. . .
Of teach me to fully live
Of close the old door and forgive.
Love is more than stopping the ache.
It's re-living our childhood wounds.
It's risking. Our hearts are at stake.
It's drastically changing our lives
Stretching way beyond limits
Healing wounds with love in our eyes.
Do we know... because of the love in our
    days
Is the way we start and the way we end
Or do we know from our free-standing ways?
That each is a bridge so willing to bend
Stretched between the bad times and the
    good.
                    —Natalie Tyler

THROUGH THIS JUNGLE OF DELIGHT

We disappear into the jungle
Along our well-worn path
Anticipating our secret beach.
We won't tell you where—
We want it to ourselves.
Up ahead it's lighter
The color of the sand
Pushes into the dark forest
Pulls us forward.
We come out onto the soft sand
Stand for a moment
Looking across the waves to forever.
Begin the tasks —set up chairs,
Mats for books and water
Lotion to keep the life-giving sun
From killing us too soon.
We settle in beside each other
In perfect peace.
For one more precious day
The beach is ours.

—Natalie Tyler & John Tyler
written together April, 1997

—Notes—

—Notes—

PART II

HOW TO DO IT

"The next message is right where you are."
—Ram Dass

5

He Says, She Says—Loving Communication

"Every loving thought is true. Everything else is an appeal for healing and help, regardless of the form it takes."1
—A Course in Miracles

THE COUPLE WHO LEFT THERAPY TOO SOON

>Please put down your book, she says.
>I just want to finish this chapter, he says.
>Please turn off the TV, she says.
>I'll use ear phones, he says.
>Could we please just talk, she says.
>For how long (with a groan), he says.
>I need some connection, she says.
>Call a girlfriend, he says.
>After the divorce
>She's sadder and lonelier
>There's no one to hear her complaints.
>He's relieved
>He doesn't have to talk.
>—Natalie Tyler

"I've never had a couple come to me and say, 'I want a divorce, my partner understands me.'"—Warren Farrell, *The Myths of Male Power*.

© Randy Glasbergen, Reprinted with Permission

Communication is the bottom line in all relationships. The ability to communicate is the ability to express what we are thinking and feeling in such a way that our partner can just listen, hear, and understand it. Communication is the single most important factor determining what happens in our relationships. Effective communication, the accurate sharing of significant information about each other and about our ideas, is the cement that holds a relationship together. We create time each day to be alone with each other. It encourages a natural flow of information. Believe it or not, some couples hardly talk to each other, except to complain. Some couples talk—both at the same time—but rarely listen. Listening is the most important element of communication.

HE SAYS, SHE SAYS—LOVING COMMUNICATION 93

© David Sipress, Reprinted with Permission

Successful relationships are built on communication. One couple we saw for several weeks finally learned how to communicate. During one of our frustrating early appointments, I asked them to tape a typical evening of conversation so they could hear themselves and learn.

With their permission, I present: "A Cozy Evening at Home with Sue and Dick." They are sitting in the living room, Dick with a crossword puzzle and TV schedule, Sue with her latest novel.

Dick: "Did you stop and get the tickets for the concert Saturday night? Did you pick up the book I ordered for my sister at Borders?"

Sue (at the same time): "I haven't gotten a babysitter for Saturday night, so maybe we should just stay home and have the Coopers over."

Dick: "Do you want to go for dinner before the concert? You say the Coopers are going with us?"

Sue: "Dick, that's not what I said, and anyhow Ricky doesn't really like Betsy. He says she yells."

Dick: "Oh, there's a movie on tonight I want to watch."

Sue: "What about Saturday night?"

Dick: "No, it's on tonight."

Sue: "Ricky will be home from baseball practice any minute. Can't we decide this?"

Dick: (unintelligible mumbling as he turns on the TV)

Sue: "I hate you. I always have!"
Ricky runs through the door.
Ricky: "Mom! Dad! Can Noah sleep over Saturday night?"
Sue starts crying hysterically and runs from the room.
Ricky: "Dad, what's wrong with Mom?"
Dick: "Huh? I think she's upset about something. I don't know. That's the nature of the beast."
Ricky: (sounding scared) "What beast?"
Now everybody starts yelling.

We can't *not* communicate. We're always communicating in some fashion. But in order to have a satisfying relationship, we must be able to communicate accurately, not only about the practical realities of the objective world, but also about the subjective realities of our inner world—our feelings and perceptions, our hopes and fears, our values and goals. To do this we must:
• Be in touch with what we feel and believe and want.
• Take the risk of confiding that information.
• And use all of the verbal and non-verbal signals necessary to communicate that information so clearly that our partner will understand.

Unless we know what we're feeling and are prepared to be honest about it, we can unconsciously confuse the issue by sending contradictory messages, with our words saying one thing while our tone of voice, facial expression, or body posture says another.

HE SAYS, SHE SAYS—LOVING COMMUNICATION

© Dr. Trudy True, Reprinted with Permission

There is nothing good or bad about thoughts and feelings—they just are. The only way you can understand yourself, be creative, and grow is to be in touch with your feelings and to accept them. When you share your feelings with your partner, three things happen: you like yourself more, others like you more, and you like others more. When you erect walls of phoniness, secrecy, and hypocrisy, you create fear, suspicion, and dislike. Effective communication is a requirement for effective problem solving and for having healthy relationships with friends, co-workers, husbands, wives, and children.

Good communication is direct, honest, clear and precise, and always respectful to your partner. Always remember that your partner is entitled to his own beliefs and feelings, even if they are different from yours.

It's important to communicate even what is difficult to say, to foster a closer understanding and a true union with your partner. It's also important to ask questions when you're not certain you understand. Intimacy is a matter of choice rather than chance. Secrets don't allow intimacy, so say it, and say it in a soft, tactful, gentle manner.

© Edgar Argo, Reprinted with Permission

Many couples have the most difficulty dealing with anger in relationships. They do not know how to express their anger because they are afraid it will destroy their love and drive their partner away. But we need to learn to communicate all of our feelings in ways that are not destructive, because suppressed feelings leak out anyway. We reveal our feelings in our expressions, in our movements, and in the closeness or distance we maintain in our relationship. Adrienne Rich says, "That which is unspoken becomes unspeakable."

HE SAYS, SHE SAYS—LOVING COMMUNICATION

© 1993, Mark Stivers, Reprinted with Permission

Linda K. Acitelli, research psychologist at the University of Michigan's Institute for Social Research, found that men who talk about their marriages tend to have happier wives than men who are more close-mouthed, and they stay happy even if men discuss negative feelings. The author says wives' identities tend to be closely linked to their relationships—so talking about marriage is the same as talking about themselves. The findings are based on two studies. In the first, couples who read fictional accounts of marriages thought that couples were happiest when their stories ended in "relationship talk." The fictional wives were perceived as happy whether the talk was positive or negative.

©John Grimes, Reprinted with Permission

In the second study, 300 couples who had been married for three years were more likely to be happy if they talked freely about the relationship in the first year of the marriage—and especially if the husbands did their share of the talking. The more a husband talks about the marital relationship, according to the study, "the greater his adjustment to the marriage—probably because he was getting problems he was concerned about out into the open—so they both were happier."

©Callahan, Reprinted with Permission
Distributed by Levin Represents

Talking clearly and openly, and the ability to listen clearly and openly, are both required. We need to be able to take in with interest, with empathy and with understanding what the other person shares. To speak on our own behalf without alienating the other person is crucial, and *so is listening*. Assumptions need to be recognized

HE SAYS, SHE SAYS—LOVING COMMUNICATION

and checked out. So much of what goes wrong in relationships results from misunderstandings. Richard Moss says, "The greatest gift we can give one another is the quality of our attention."

"Federal Bureau of Feelings, sir. It seems that last night you neglected to ask your wife how her day was. You have the right to remain silent."

Reprinted with Permission, © The New Yorker Collection, 1990 Tom Cheney from cartoonbank.com, All Rights Reserved

DAILY TEMPERATURE READING

Couples who do the Daily Temperature Reading* every day say that the change in their relationship feels miraculous—just by communicating regularly. The Daily Temperature Reading helps couples to stay current with each other, feel heard, and know each other better. Done properly, it keeps you centered and on track, no one goes off on a tangent or starts talking in circles, and arguments

* The Daily Temperature Reading was developed by Virginia Satir. We changed the third item from "Puzzles" to "Questions" and the fourth from "Complaints" to "Observations with Request for Change."

don't escalate. A Daily Temperature Reading usually takes 10 to 20 minutes. It's preferable for the two people to be facing each other, and on the same level, with no TV, radio, phone, or other interruptions.

Decide who will be the first speaker, and who will be the attentive listener who doesn't interrupt *no matter what*. The Daily Temperature Reading has five parts:

1. Appreciations. One person starts by saying, "Some things I appreciate (or love) about you are..." Tell her some things you appreciate about her (not just things she does, but also her looks, her personality, and her character), and about life in general. These strokes encourage us and improve our self-esteem. Regular strokes help us to work through difficulties with good will, and make us feel loved, accepted, important, special, and hopeful. After hearing Appreciations, the listener opens her heart and ears more fully to hear all the rest of what you have to say.

2. New Information. Share one statement of new information. Your partner just listens. You can share anything you want her to know—about yourself, your work, children, or friends. It may be important or frivolous—just share it! Sharing new information keeps us current and connected with each other.

3. Questions. This can be a question you want to ask your partner, information that you want or need, or anything that puzzles you about your partner or your relationship. It's important to ask, not ass-u-me (make an "ass" out of "u" and "me"). Your partner can then speak by answering the question in one sentence.

4. Observations with Requests for Change. It's okay to complain, but you must tell your partner the specific change you want instead of what she is doing.

Present your observation clearly, directly and specifically, at a time when your partner is available to hear it (after she's heard appreciations and received new information). Include a specific request for the change you want. Your partner just listens, digests the request, and doesn't answer during the exercise at this time.

5. Wishes, Hopes, and Dreams. Sharing dreams helps a couple build a common future together. You'll find out if you share the same goals and learn to know each other on a deeper level. Then reverse roles, so your partner has a turn to fully express herself and receive the listening we all crave. After you've both had a turn, give each other a hug of appreciation and say that phrase that doesn't get said enough, "Thank you!"

The only time the listener speaks is to answer the question in #3. Appreciations can be numerous, but then only one statement of new information, one question, one complaint with request for change, and one wish or hope or dream, so as not to overwhelm your partner. If you do the Daily Temperature Reading *every day* you will feel satisfied with one sentence for each of the five points, and you'll notice that your partner, who is still basking in the appreciations, will not become overwhelmed and defensive, especially since she knows that she will have a turn. Feelings won't build up to unmanageable proportions and you won't lose your thoughts. Besides, receiving daily appreciations builds your self-esteem, helps you to remember the positive characteristics of your partner, and generates good will between you.

Some people start the day with a Daily Temperature Reading, some do it after work before supper, and some before bed to clear things for a good night's sleep. Many families do a Daily Temperature Reading around the dinner table nightly. Children love it! Some agencies, small companies, and large corporations use the Daily

Temperature Reading during their staff meetings, and we have taught teachers and youth center directors who use it with the children very successfully!

"There is only one rule for being a good talker: Learn to listen."—Christopher Morley

Theologian Paul Tillich says, "The first law of love is to listen, to want to listen, to do deliberate listening without an agenda." When one person speaks, the other listens. After that, the other gets to respond. The empathic listening format is used throughout.

"Most of the time we don't communicate, we just take turns talking."—Dr. Robert Anthony

Unity Church minister Rev. Judy Grimes says, "We have two ears and one mouth, because we need to listen twice as much as we talk."

PEANUTS reprinted by permission of United Feature Syndicte, Inc.

MAD SAD SCARED GLAD

Most of our clients and students say "Mad-Sad-Scared-Glad" is their favorite communication tool. It helps you to get in touch with your feelings when you are feeling grouchy, grumpy, out of sorts, or even depressed, and you don't know why. It also helps your partner to know what you are feeling, so he doesn't assume it's about him and make himself feel guilty, and to know that he doesn't have to fix it. It's just you expressing your feelings, emptying all of your pent-up emotions and freeing your heart, mind, and body so you can be a full participant in the present day or evening, aware of the reasons for being glad.

Always begin by asking permission: "Will you do Mad-Sad-Scared-Glad with me?"

Start with **MAD**:

Partner #1 asks: "What are you mad about?"
Partner #2 answers with the first thing that comes up.
Partner #1: "Thank you. What else are you mad about?"
Partner #2 answers with the next thing that comes up.
Partner #1: "Thank you. What else are you mad about?"
Partner #2 answers.
Partner #1 keeps asking until there is nothing more #2 is mad about.
Partner #1 asks: "If you were mad about something else, what would it be?"
Partner #2 answers one last thing.
Partner #1: "Thank you.

Then move to **SAD**:

Partner #1 asks: "What are you *sad* about?"
Partner #2 answers as before, and repeats format until #2 says, "That's all."
Partner #1 asks: "If you were sad about something else, what would it be?"
Partner #2 answers one last thing.
Partner #1: "Thank you."

Then move to **SCARED**:

Partner #1 asks: "What are you *scared* about?"
Partner #2 answers as before, and repeats format until #2 says, "That's all."
Partner #1 asks: "If you were scared about something else, what would it be?"
Partner #2 answers one last thing.
Partner #1: "Thank you."

Then move to **GLAD**.

This one is done a little differently:
Partner #1 asks: "What are you glad about?" only once.
Partner #2 lists all the things they're glad about without stopping.
Partner #1: "Thank you."

ENDING:

Partner #2: "Thank you for listening to my feelings."
Partner #1: "Thank you for sharing your feelings with me."
Partners #1 and #2: Give each other hugs.

No conversation takes place. That would interfere with this important clearing process. After one partner finishes, switch roles. Remember, as the listener it's important that you keep saying, "What are you mad (or sad or scared) about?" until the other person says, "That's all." Then you ask one final time, "If you were mad (or sad or scared) about something else, what would it be?" Sometimes we cover up our feelings so much that we are not in touch with the deepest, most important feeling that's blocking our energy, and this last question helps us to uncover that and express it. Also remember to say "Thank you" after each answer to your question. Then

HE SAYS, SHE SAYS—LOVING COMMUNICATION

your partner knows you've heard her, and you know there's nothing you have to do about it except listen and ask.

Always ending with Glad helps you to remember, after unloading, about the good things in life. The Mads, Sads, Scares, and Glads can be about anything, not just the two of you. And love can be remembered if some of the glads are about each other and your life together.

All of these tools are done with permission only. Always ask, "Will you do a Daily Temperature Reading with me?" or "Will you do Mad-Sad-Scared-Glad with me?" To keep a happy marriage and the communication lines open, whenever you can, say "Yes." If it's impossible at the time, the best thing to say is, "I'm sorry honey, I can't now," and then offer a more convenient time as soon as possible, and definitely before the night is over. Hey kids, don't go to bed mad or stuff your feelings or stifle your ideas. We hope you'll clear everything each day before entering the sacred space of your bedroom temple. More about that later, I promise!

© Peter Mueller, Reprinted with Permission

Barry and Joyce Vissell say, "The highest purpose of communicating is communing, which is becoming one with each other." This is a further extension of communication, beyond just sharing thoughts and feelings. This is a deep recognition of another person's being. This sometimes takes place in silence, maybe while looking into each other's eyes, making love, walking in the woods, or listening to music together. Suddenly we feel touched and seen, not as a personality but in the depth of our being. This kind of communication can happen with or without words. If clear verbal communication is used regularly, this deeper, spontaneous (sometimes silent, sometimes with a few gentle words) communion takes place at the level of mind, heart, and soul. This deeper form of intimacy enables us to overcome our separateness and engenders a total union between two intimates.

© Nicole Hollander, 1958, Reprinted with Permission

WATERFALL

Feelings are energy, and energy has to be utilized. Storing feelings causes sickness, pain, low energy, or depression and a feeling of distance from your partner. Sometimes it's useful to cry and remove emotional tensions. This helpful exercise allows you to do just that in a way that is positive and productive and brings you closer to your partner. The partner who feels like crying says to her loved one, "Will you hear my Waterfall?" The dear one says, "For how long?" The sad one says, "Five minutes" (or 10, or 15 — whatever she thinks she needs). Anyone can listen to crying for an agreed upon short time, and it's usually all the person needs. He holds her like a baby and comforts her with caresses and a few words. She feels better, thanks him, and appreciates his caring tenderness.

MORE GUIDELINES FOR CONSCIOUS COMMUNICATION

Listen for what a person is *not* saying as well as what is said. Check out what you are hearing by telling your partner as exactly as you can what you heard her say, including the attitudes and feelings you heard expressed. Use similar words to your partner's, and don't change her meaning. Do not substitute your own message, or evaluate, sympathize, give your opinion, offer advice, analyze, or question. Simply report back what you heard.

In light of these guidelines, how much time have you spent really listening to others this week? When did you experience the "duet dance" of listening?

Doonesbury, © G.B. Trudeau, Reprinted wih Permission of Universal Press Syndicate. All rights reserved.

"The quality of your interpersonal relationships... sculpts your personality—determining in large measure whether you can become the kind of person you want to be. Only you can decide whether it is worth the diligent and disciplined effort which it, like any complex skill, requires." —Bernard Guerney, Jr., Ph.D.

"The point of a fish hook is to catch a fish. Once you've caught a fish you can dispense with the fish hook. The point of a rabbit trap is to catch a rabbit. Once you've caught a rabbit you can dispense with the rabbit trap. The point of words is to catch meaning. Once you've gotten the meaning you can dispense with the words. Where oh where can I find a man who has gotten the meaning so I can have a word with him?"
—Chuang-Tse-Tsu

© Callahan, Reprinted with Permission

—Notes—

6

Closer Through Conflict

"Those who offer peace to everyone have found a home in Heaven the world cannot destroy."[1]
—**A Course in Miracles**

Our motto in our marriage is, "Love is more important than being right." The next time you engage in verbal combat, say these seven powerful words and notice the miracle: you have the power to diffuse anger and transform energy. When you add these seven calming words to the other phrases that steer your relationship on the road to health and happiness, you will both win. Here are some more important phrases to remember:
• One word—"Yes".
• Two words—"I'm sorry" and "Thank you".
• Three words—"I love you".
• Four words—"You might be right," and "Oops, no big deal".

Remember—the best way to have the last word is to apologize.

Alan Cohen says, "Every minus is half of a plus waiting for a stroke of veritable awareness," and A Course in Miracles says, "It is when judgment ceases that healing occurs."[2] Blame is a convenient way to avoid looking inside and taking responsibility for our own issues. It is a way to distance ourselves from each other to cover up our fear of intimacy. A Course in Miracles says, "I am never upset for the reason I think."[3] What we are angry about is most often a projection of our own issues, not our partner. The real issue is our internal reaction to our partner. Anger is a symptom of discomfort, so we look for someone else to blame to avoid the pain of working through our blocks, addictions, and fears. Speaking of fear, underneath anger there is always fear. We would not feel angry if we were not fearful about something. A Course in Miracles says, "Fear is not of the present, but only of the past and future, which do not exist."[4]

Nancy was angry with Phil for dancing too long with another woman at the party. She was afraid he would be so turned on that he would have an affair and then leave her. Sol was angry with Janet for talking to her mother on the phone so long. He was afraid she would be tired, and they would not make love. Claire was mad at Steve for not doing his share of child care. She was afraid their kids would grow up like she did—ignored by her father and feeling unimportant.

When we take the time to discover what we are really afraid of, we convert anger into self-knowledge. When we communicate our fears instead of our anger, our partner is more likely to understand. Then we can ask for reasonable changes. We can say to our Beloved, "Thank you for being my dear teacher and showing me this." Converting anger into awareness of the fear underneath is like turning lead into gold.

When couples begin the Mad, Sad, Scared, Glad exercise in Chapter 5 with, "What are you mad about?" they usually start off with small frustrations, then progress to mild irritations, and finally get to deep anger that they were not aware of. Sometimes they have unresolved childhood issues, or even abuse they have forgotten, but the pain remains. Intense rage is *always* rooted in childhood injuries. In many instances our caretakers, who meant well, were not equipped to deal with what happened and what was needed. When we grow up the rage is always there, just under the surface of our aware-

CLOSER THROUGH CONFLICT   113

ness, until someone touches it. Then we often react the way we did as children. When we learn to look into the fear beneath the rage, we can bring it to the surface and discharge it in a safe environment with a nurturing spouse or therapist.

Our feelings are just as much a part of us as our nose, our mouth or our eyes. It is not healthy to ignore our feelings and hold them inside. They will leak out anyway. Anger leaks out in ongoing episodes of irritability, harsh tones, and mean words toward people who are innocent recipients of our historical rage. When we stop playing the blame game, we have the energy to look inside and begin to resolve our issues. Remember the old saying, "It takes two to tango." Well, when a couple comes to us for therapy, we always look for the system they have developed *together*—how each touches off the other's childhood wounds.

©David Sipress, Reprinted with Permission

Paul and Suki came in blaming each other. She said he criticized her for every little thing and demanded perfection. He said she could not do anything right and was always late, and that she was distant with him. Of course, Suki was late—she would put off coming home to Paul's criticisms as long as possible. Then he would criticize her for being late, and they were in the vicious circle! He demanded perfection, and she made herself so nervous, trying to live up to his standards, that she had trouble functioning. Of course she felt distant from this "mean daddy figure." Suki had been afraid of her own strict father, and she unconsciously became attracted to a man as rigid as her father (her IMAGO—see Chapter 4), hoping this time she would be careful and do things right. She went along "trying" for years, not expressing her anger or fear, or asking for behavior changes, equality and respect, or seeking couple therapy. Paul spent his childhood taking care of his alcoholic mother and trying to force her to do things right. He never knew when she would come home. He continued those early unconscious patterns with Suki. By the time they came to us, their family system in their marriage was so deeply ingrained that it took long-term therapy (the kind insurance companies do not understand and will not pay for) to heal the wounds.

This was not about Paul being the bad guy and Suki the innocent victim. When they stopped blaming each other and started to look inside to learn how they each kept the system going, and each began to take responsibility for their part, everything changed for the better. Then we taught them how to help heal each other's childhood wounds.

It's important to remember that *no one can make us feel anything*. We unconsciously decide what to feel according to the feeling we became accustomed to in childhood. Transactional Analysis calls this habitual feeling our racket. Some of the most common rackets are

CLOSER THROUGH CONFLICT

anger, fear, worry, sadness, hurt, physical symptoms, and fatigue. The same thing can happen to each of us, and we will each respond differently—we will choose our racket feeling, whether it is appropriate to the circumstances or not.

When John and I were driving to Key West on the Ocean Highway, the bridge fell out. We were stuck in traffic, a line of cars as far as we could see ahead and behind. It was a hot, sunny day, and there was no possible way to turn around unless we had an amphibious vehicle that we could slide off the narrow passageway into the ocean, or a flying machine that would take us over all the other cars and beyond to Cuba. Well, all of us in those hundreds of cars were in the same predicament, and alas, each person had a different reaction (their racket). It took an hour for the repairmen to arrive and three hours to fix the bridge so we could continue. We were trapped in our stand-still ordeal for four hours. The man in the green jeep in front of us meditated for four hours and told us it was a peak spiritual experience of enlightenment.

Two cars down in a white Mercedes, we heard a couple screaming at each other, using words I had not heard before, or since. When we opened the Key West newspaper the next day, we read that the woman sued for divorce, after arriving at their destination—the southernmost point in the country, and the end of their marriage. The newspaper also announced the engagement of a couple who had just met. They had spent the four hours bonding and falling in love. Another man made himself feel so hopeless, he dove into the ocean from his red convertible and drowned. The couple in the bright blue Chevy behind us shared a bottle of crisp, cold Chardonnay from their ice chest, and we had a memorable time listening to their collection of Simon and Garfunkel tapes, and our Ella Fitzgerald, Joan Baez and Pat Metheny tapes. We told jokes and shared our life stories. We became best friends and still visit each other over the miles and the years.

Then there was the time when Sir Tallness (husbands need lots of pet names! Wives too!) and I returned from teaching therapists in China, after a twenty hour plane trip back to Massachusetts, where we lived and practiced in "The Happy Valley." We were exhausted and went to take a half-hour nap before it was time for our regular Thursday night favorite therapy group. As you can imagine the "half-hour" turned into deep dream time, and downstairs in our therapy room our clients waited for their therapists.

Each reacted in a different way. Julie, with a worry racket said, "I know they were killed in a plane accident," paced the floor, wrung her hands and obsessed—obsessing is the opposite of thinking. Obsessing about the same thing over and over keeps us from logic or moving forward with new thoughts. Marcie went into her anger racket and shouted, "If they can't even be here on time, they shouldn't be therapists. I'm leaving!" Jake to the rescue! "Maybe they were tired after the trip and fell asleep by mistake. I'll go up and wake them." Mick, with the scare racket, grabbed Jake's arm and said, "You'd better not go up into their private quarters. They might get mad." Jake came up anyway, awakened us, and we came down and had the best therapy group of our life. Everyone was fully feeling their feelings, we related their rackets back to what it reminded each of them from childhood, and, voila!—everyone moved further along in their therapy and felt better, and we felt better, too—and un-jet-lagged!

Another memorable time was when we had a weekend therapy marathon. People had shared their deepest issues and worked through blocks they had been carrying for years. We all felt so bonded and so close to each other as we stood in a group hug circle and sang Molly Scott's "We are all one family." Crash! A three car accident on the corner in front of our house! The tight circle broke and each person reacted in his own way. Mary cried, Ann screamed and Alice prayed. Sam called the police, Barry went out to direct traffic, and darling Robert went out to comfort the children in the cars. I could have told you in advance what they each would have done.

©Peter Mueller, Reprinted with Permission

Circumstances do not control our actions. We all have the potential to be in charge of our feelings, our actions, and our lives—to be free. We decide how to feel and what actions to take. A Course in Miracles says, "I can be hurt by nothing but my thoughts."[5]

One of the ways to handle our anger and at the same time take responsibility for our own feelings is to use the phrase, *"I make myself feel* (angry, sad, scared, glad) *when you* (describe behavior)." For example, "I make myself feel angry when you arrive late. In the future will you come home on time or call and let me know you'll be late?"

Reprinted with special permission of King Features Syndicate.

If you are angry longer than ten minutes after you have expressed your anger, you are rubber banding back to your past, connecting with a childhood wound that needs healing, or mistreatments in other relationships that still need closure. A Course in Miracles says, "If [attack] is not relinquished entirely, it is not relinquished at all."[6]

CLOSER THROUGH CONFLICT

©Jennifer Berman, Reprinted with Permission

Men and women cannot "settle things" by the old fashioned kind of arguing and talking in circles, by criticizing each other, and dishing out verbal abuse and put-downs. If you want to heal your relationship, then you must learn to use the language of the harp, not the sword. What a difference when you affirm the other person and express your love and devotion. The harp heals and binds together. The sword wounds and cuts asunder!

Have you ever had a bad fight, and you could not even remember how it started or what it was all about? We all have. We can feel closer to each other by using the tools on the following pages instead of the old-fashioned criticism, yelling, name-calling, threatening divorce, slamming doors, talking in circles, nagging or withdrawing. As A Course in Miracles says, "There is another way of looking at the world."[7]

©David Sipress, Reprinted with Permission

It is normal to be angry with each other sometimes—after all you come from different childhood backgrounds, and you have different ideas, needs and values. Those differences are bound to come into conflict from time to time. But it's not OK to lash out at each other. This surprise attack startles your partner, he reacts—either defensively or aggressively—and you are off on a roller coaster ride of misunderstanding and hurt. When we feel threatened, we unconsciously respond the way we learned to deal with attacks as children—we either counterattack or withdraw.

CLOSER THROUGH CONFLICT

STIVERS

©Mark Stivers, Reprinted with Permission

We hereby present some better ways developed by George Bach, author of *The Intimate Enemy*, improved by us at the request of and with our PAIRS® couples:

HAIRCUT

The Haircut is used to release anger at your partner. So the first requirement is to make it safe for *both* of you to deal with anger. We do this by imposing these very important rules: First, you ask his permission to express your anger at him, and he must agree or commit to an agreed upon later time. In this way he becomes a willing participant in the process. Second, you set a time limit, so he knows he will not have to listen to your anger indefinitely. He can stay present while you discharge your anger, and you can effectively discharge it because you know he is hearing what you are upset about. Third, once you have expressed your anger fully in this way, you agree never to mention the incident again.

Here are the steps to the Haircut:
PARTNER #1: "May I give you a Haircut?"
PARTNER #2: "Yes—for how long?"
PARTNER #1: "For ___ minutes." (not more than 5 minutes)
PARTNER #2: "All right"
PARTNER #1: **VENT VENT VENT**
(#2 - **NO TALKING AT ALL—JUST LISTEN,** even if you disagree with what #1 is saying.)
(At end of requested time, or when #1 is through, whichever comes first)
PARTNER #2: "How do I get out of the Doghouse?"
(**DOGHOUSE RELEASE**—some apology or other action that will get #2 off the hook. Designed to replace punishment and blame with something more pleasurable, from a simple "I'm sorry" or "Give me a Hug" to a favor or task that will help #1 forgive and forget about what she was angry about).
PARTNER #1: Tells #2 what he can do to "get out of the Doghouse".
PARTNER #2: Usually agrees to do what is necessary to get out of the Doghouse.
(If #2 does not agree, you need to look at whether this is a power struggle.)
PARTNER #1: "Thank you for listening."
PARTNER #2: "Thank you for letting go of your anger" (so it won't contaminate the relationship). Then give each other a hug.

"I have invented this situation as I see it."[8]
—A Course in Miracles

CLOSER THROUGH CONFLICT

| Rather than seeing someone as attacking... | I can see them as fearful and giving me a call of help for love. |

Reprinted with permission.

"My thoughts are images I have made."⁹
—A Course in Miracles

VESUVIUS

When you are angry about things in general, not only your partner, you use the Vesuvius. You ask for permission and the process is time limited like the Haircut, but there is no Doghouse Release.

PARTNER #1: "Will you hear my Vesuvius?"
PARTNER #2: "Yes—for how long?"
PARTNER #1: "For ___ minutes." (not more than 5 minutes)
PARTNER #2: "All right"

PARTNER #1: **VENT   VENT   VENT**
PARTNER #1: "Thank you for listening."
PARTNER #2: "Thank you for letting go of your anger.
Both partners hug.

©Nicole Hollander, Reprinted withPermission

CLOSER THROUGH CONFLICT 125

Sweeping resentment under the rug may feel safe for the moment, but it keeps us stuck and distances us from each other. As John A. Shedd said, "A ship in the harbor is safe—but that is not what ships are for." Marriage is a learning process, and it can be a powerful healing lifestyle if we use the challenges as opportunities to understand ourselves and each other, to connect soul to soul, soul with spirit.

©PEANUTS reprinted by permission of United Feature Syndicate, Inc.

What gets in the way more than anything else is our family history. Here are ways to discover the styles you learned to use as children. Ask yourself these questions:
• How did my parents argue?
• Who was most likely to start the fight?
• What was my parent responding to?
• How did the perpetrator or victim stimulate the other parent to argue?
• What was the purpose of my parent starting the fight?
• Who do my children think start our fights? What would give them that idea?
• How did I feel when my parents fought? How do I think my children feel? How do I know?
• What can I do differently the next time that could prevent the escalation? What would make it worse?

Share your realizations with your partner, and then discuss how you can change them to more constructive and loving ways. The next time you have a fight, use this

exercise to understand the escalation:
- Take turns describing what each of you experienced just prior to the argument.
- Go back to the last time you both were feeling good about each other. Then discuss who first became aware of feeling uncomfortable, tense, upset, distant, etc.? What did each of you then do?
- Think back over your arguments or fights. What triggers your upset feelings? Is there a general theme that characterizes your feelings? Have you felt this way before, in other relationships, or with parents, teachers, or employers?
- What physical sensations do you experience when you are upset with your partner? Where in your body? Now describe the feeling—its size, shape, color, and density. Notice whether the feeling changes or shifts as you focus your attention on it.
- Is the feeling like anything you've felt before? Notice any similarities between current feelings and childhood experiences.

©Peter Mueller, Reprinted with Permission

CLOSER THROUGH CONFLICT

Sometimes we can accept our partner's shortcomings and idiosyncrasies as just endearing habits that make him unique, and let it be "Oops, no big deal." Epictetus said two thousand years ago, "If you do not wish to be prone to anger, do not feed the habit." A Course In Miracles says, "Those who see themselves as whole make no demands."[10]

We push people away by our need to control, judge, or manipulate. Surrendering and transforming that need—sometimes it takes therapy—is the key to transformation. We may no longer get our own way, but as the Sufi teaching says, "When the heart weeps for what it has lost, the soul laughs for what it has found."

I am going to tell you the deep dark secret every couple needs to know that can keep knock-down (verbally), drag out (nagging and going over the same thing many times) fights from happening: remember that only one person should go crazy at a time. If one of you goes crazy with anger, the other needs to be the calm patient sponge.

A Course In Miracles says, "Only infinite patience produces immediate effects."[11] One of us can stay with the truth of love and stay in his right mind, and that makes all the difference.

We cannot agree on everything—we're not Siamese twins. It is natural to have different viewpoints in some areas. When we cannot agree, we can meet each other halfway; we can each accept part rather than demand everything. To do this, we use the Fair Fight for Change:

FAIR FIGHT FOR CHANGE

PARTNER #1 asks, "Will you join with me in a Fair Fight for Change?"

PARTNER #2 agrees.

PARTNER #1 MEDITATE—Go inside and define the issue clearly to yourself.

PARTNER #1 STATE YOUR COMPLAINT—a *specific behavior* your partner does.

PARTNER #2 FEEDBACK—Repeat complaint, *without editing*.

PARTNER #1 DESCRIBE how this behavior affects you. Talk about your feelings: "I make myself feel (angry, sad, scared, upset, etc.) when you do that."

PARTNER #2 FEEDBACK—Repeat after every one or two sentences what you heard, without editing.

PARTNER #1 CONTINUE to give information until all feelings have been expressed. Then thank #2 for listening.

PARTNER #2 VALIDATION—"I can understand how you could feel that way."

PARTNER #1 MEDITATE on the specific way(s) you want your partner to change *their behavior—not* the way they think or feel.

PARTNER #1 DESCRIBE *behavioral* change you want in as few words as possible. "What I would like is . . ."

PARTNER #2 FEEDBACK—Repeat request, again without editing.

PARTNER #1 REQUEST—"Are you willing to do that?"

PARTNER #2 MEDITATE—Ask yourself "Do I want to make this change, and under what conditions? What will it mean if I say 'Yes'?" "Do I need to set conditions?"

PARTNER #2 RESPONSE—Respond with "Yes" / "Yes with conditions" / "No"

PARTNER #1 CONFIRM what you heard #2 agree to do and under what conditions. *Make sure you both understand and agree to the terms.*

CLOSURE—Commit to action and thank each other with a hug.
WRITE DOWN AGREEMENT AND BOTH SIGN IT

If you handle your differences constructively, using the Communication skills described in chapter 5—the Daily Temperature Reading, Mad, Sad, Scared, Glad—and the Conflict Resolution tools in this chapter—the Haircut, Vesuvius, and Fair Fight For Change—you will heal, grow, and deepen your connection. Sam Keen says, "The conflict in marriage is the forge of the spirit." If necessary we can take a time out, but the healthy way is to resolve the issue completely using a Fair Fight For Change. As Robert Frost said, "The best way out is through."

"You have no idea of the tremendous release and deep peace that comes from meeting yourself and your brother totally without judgment.[12] Judgment and love are opposites. From one comes all the sorrows of the world. But from the other comes the peace of God himself."[13]—A Course in Miracles

—Notes—

7
CARING BEHAVIORS

"The fragrance always remains in the hand that gives the rose."
—Mahatma Ghandi

©Marian Henley, Reprinted with Permission

"To keep a lamp burning, we must keep putting oil in it."—Mother Teresa

LOVE-IN

Only a lover can conceive a Love-In.
Only a lover has love enough
    to share a Love-In with another lover.
We think we say words and create the love
Love is the source of all the love words
Love is the source of all the love.
Our love feeds on itself
    grows in different ways
on different days.
Grows red hearts and tulips
    on Valentine's Day.

My love for you fills my mouth
    with "I love you."
                  —John Tyler

"Receiving is very different from the ego-consciousness of 'getting.' It is the conscious activity of opening the heart to draw in the Divine from another. Receiving is one of the highest gifts we can give to one another."
—Barry & Joyce Vissell

TOUCHING

We ride in the car together to Connecticut
    to see my mother, your good friend.
Your hand is on my leg most of the way.
Sometimes you use your hand to turn
    the page you've just read
    then return it to my thigh.
I feel the warmth of your hand
    through blue denims
    reassuring, not sexual
    letting me know you know I'm there
    driving as you're reading
    the way you always let me know
    you know about me
    with gentle touch
    or fierce caress.
I'm never in doubt about
    whether you care.

—John Tyler

    The heart of intimacy is a willingness to keep exchanging yourself with your other through an ever-deepening giving and receiving, until separateness melts into spiritual union. Aldous Huxley once remarked that it was a bit embarrassing to get to the end of his life and have no more profound advice than "be a little kinder." Stephen Vincent Benet said, "Life is not lost by dying; life is lost minute by minute, day by dragging day, in all the thousand small uncaring ways."

    Rev. Judy Grimes said in the Unity Church of Maui Newsletter:

    "We know one cannot give without receiving or receive without giving. Both giving and receiving are continued in one action; they are two ends of the same process, like the very breath we give and receive. Although the atmosphere around us is full of air, we cannot draw a fresh breath until we release (give) the one we are holding."

Ursula LeGuin says, "Love doesn't just sit there like a stone: it has to be made like bread, remade all the time, made new." That's what Caring Behaviors are all about. Caring Behaviors are important, and they make a difference! This age we live in offers us an abundance of information. The different cultures and people in the world possess incredible wisdom that could heal our planet. We all know the simple truths about kindness and giving. We have all the knowledge. We need only practice and use what we already know. A positive phrase, thought or act spreads light throughout our world. We can help scatter the seeds of love and plant joy in each other's hearts by carefully choosing our actions and thoughts.

IN A CONSCIOUS RELATIONSHIP, PARTNERS GIVE CARING BEHAVIORS DAILY

Caring behaviors are the life blood of our relationship. These small, frequent acts of sensitivity, kindness and caring let our partner know that she is important to us. Caring Behaviors range from a warm "Welcome home honey!" on returning home, to a phone call during the day, to special gifts and cards at birthdays and anniversaries, to a back rub or a foot rub. They tell our partner that she is important and that our relationship is important. Practicing caring behaviors is necessary to sustain a loving relationship. A Course in Miracles says, "Never forget you give but to yourself. Who understands what giving means must laugh at the idea of sacrifice.[1] For giving and receiving are the same."[2]

CARING BEHAVIORS

CARING BEHAVIORS LIST*

Complete the sentence below in as many ways as you can by listing behaviors, words and symbols your partner is *currently* using that make you feel cared about and loved.

I feel cared about and loved when you:
1.
2.
3.
4.
5.
6.
7.
8.

"I'd rather have roses on my table than diamonds on my neck."—Emma Goldman

- **Past Behaviors:** Now recall the romantic phase of your relationship, and complete the sentence below by listing the ways your partner made you feel loved and cared about *in the past*. Be specific, descriptive, positive and quantitative (how much, how often).

I felt cared about and loved when you:
1.
2.
3.
4.
5.
6.
7.
8.

"Men as a rule love with their eyes, but women love with their ears."—Oscar Wilde

* Adapted from *Getting the Love You Want*, Harville Hendrix, Ph.D.

• **Secret Desires:** There are, perhaps, some caring and loving behaviors you have always wanted but never requested. They may come from fantasy, experience, or your image of an ideal partner. They are *secret desires.* Keeping a desire secret means you have some fear of expressing it. List your fear in the first column and your desire in the second:

I am willing to give up my fear of . . .

1.
2.
3.
4.
5.
6.
7.
8.

...and ask you to express your love by. . .

1.
2.
3.
4.
5.
6.
7.
8.

Now exchange lists. Read your partner's list carefully, and make sure you are clear about what she wants as caring behaviors. Feel free to add a caring behavior from her list if it is something you, too, would find pleasurable.

Post your partner's list at home where you will see it every morning—on the bathroom mirror, on your dresser,

CARING BEHAVIORS

or on your refrigerator. For the next week, make a point of showing how much you care by doing at least three caring behaviors on her list every day. Each evening during the Daily Temperature Reading, in your Appreciations, be sure to appreciate her for the caring behaviors she has shown you. If you have provided caring behaviors that she did not appreciate, gently call attention to them when you give your New Information during the Daily Temperature Reading. At the end of the week, talk about whether the caring behaviors have made a difference in how you feel toward each other.

A lessening of caring behaviors is often a sign that your relationship is under stress, that you are experiencing negative feelings and holding grudges. Often when partners are having difficulty in their relationship, they wait for the loving feelings to return before continuing with caring behaviors. This is backward thinking! We have found that when we practice caring behaviors, whether or not we feel loving in the moment, our feelings catch up! So take the initiative in offering acts of caring and kindness, and don't wait to see what your partner is going to do, in a tit for tat fashion.

Remember, your partner is not a mind reader. You are responsible for knowing what makes you feel loved. If you don't ask for that behavior, your partner may not think of it on his own. He cannot know what you want unless you ask. Caring behaviors nurture a relationship and create an atmosphere in which tenderness and love can thrive.

Here are some caring behaviors others have listed:
- Give me a massage
- Bring me breakfast in bed
- Ask me about my work or how I'm feeling or how my day went
- Ask me out on a date and you plan the whole evening
- Give me a long, tender kiss instead of a "hello" or "goodby" peck

- Hold my hand in the movies
- Put your arm around my shoulder or your hand on the back of my neck
- Rub my head or play with my hair
- Make dinner
- Exercise with me
- Be nice to my parents and friends
- Call during the day
- Give me love notes and cards
- Bring me flowers
- Snuggle with me in the morning before we get up

You can even include special circumstances, such as:
- When I am sick, I love it when you...
- When I am tired, please...
- When I am worried, I want...
- When I am afraid...
- When I am unhappy, please...
- For celebrations, I want...

Relationship brings spirituality down to earth and into the home. The love and care we give to others is at the heart of spirituality. There is no separation between us.

When I was a little girl in the 4th grade in Cincinnati, the teacher, Miss Satchelaben, gave us an assignment to memorize: "Appreciation is to the human heart as rain from heaven is to the plants." I've never forgotten that. Each time we lavish caring behaviors on our spouse, and anyone else for that matter, with strokes, compliments and appreciations, we're giving target strokes, which melt the walls around the heart.

It's not only what you do, but how you do it. It is important that you accept the fact that your partner is the only one who knows what she wants. I encourage you to do the caring behavior your partner has asked for, and add some of your own creative imagination to the request.

CARING BEHAVIORS

"It matters immensely. The slightest sound matters. The most momentary rhythm matters. You can do as you please, yet everything matters."—Wallace Stevens

"Do unto others as they wish, but with imagination."—Marcel Duchamp

"She puts her hand under my shirt and writes the names of flowers on my back."—Mark Strand

And remember, it's not only what you say, it's how you say it:
"Won't you come into the garden
I would like my roses to see you."—Richard Sheridan

Finally, remember the most important words and phrases that melt the armor:

- "I'm sorry."
- "Thank you."
- "You might be right."
- "Ooops, no big deal!"

"If the only prayer you ever say in your whole life is 'Thank you,' that would suffice." —Meister Eckhart

—Notes—

8
Sexuality & Sensuality
or
My Secret Fabulous Life in Paradise

TOUCHING

Our bodies, sleeping
touching lie
knee and ankle
hip and thigh
Our upper torsos
more apart
to ease the beating
of my heart.
—John Tyler

MORNING LOVE

This morning in our bedroom
there was a light show
on the ceiling
and the angels laughed.
—Natalie Tyler

You know what my Prince Charming and I do for a living?! We teach love! How's that for right livelihood? And would you like to know how we spend our busman's holidays? Read on.

Late in the afternoon at the beach, a strange magic fills the air with a calming, quiet, peaceful, powerfully spiritual energy. It almost seems—no, it does seem—as if we go into another time zone, into a space where nothing outside of here matters, and right here under our sweet-smelling pink Plumeria tree by the sea, everything matters. Often we're indoors this time of the day, communing with clients, but on this Friday—our special sacred day of the week—we're at the beach from morning until night. For us, it's better than a weekend at a spa or a fancy city hotel. It's a spiritual meditative retreat. It's our day to refresh, refuel, reorganize, re-energize, and regenerate.

In the morning, during our long beach walk, we watch a mother whale and her baby breaching close to shore. We eat our picnic lunch of Mahi Mahi sandwiches on fresh rye bread with lettuce, tomatoes, onions and avocados from our yard. Then we read our separate books in the companionable silence of the long married, occasionally broken by "Listen to this!" from one of us. After putting our books aside—his an historical novel, mine the newest psychology book—we choose Wendell Berry's *The Country of Marriage* and each read a poem aloud. Then I write while he naps. I love watching him sleep. He's in his mid-60's, when certain healthy, happy men get more handsome, and yet he looks so young and innocent: innocent of meanness, harshness, violence, greed, or selfishness. None if it has ever been part of his life, and I think I've been assigned the important job of being his guardian angel to protect his innocence.

After his cat nap, my innocent, wise, sexy gray-bearded husband awakens and returns to the world as we know it on our secluded—we won't tell you where!—

SEXUALITY & SENSUALITY OR MY SECRET FABULOUS LIFE IN PARADISE

beach on Maui. He takes our masks and flippers out of the snorkeling bag and carefully spreads anti-fogging solution on my mask and his. He does this ritual each day. He *likes* doing little things for me that I could do for myself. I bask in the Caring Behavior, glad I married a man who believes in equality, yet enjoys being a gentleman of the old school. We walk to the shore and dress for the occasion. Water angels, swimming freely, we meet our friendly turtle companions. After half an hour, we stop following them, and lo and behold, they decide to follow us! Soon we lose track of who is leading and who is following, and it becomes a long, slow, blissful, contemplative dance.

Later that evening, after dinner at our favorite romantic beachside café, we walk along Sugar Beach by the light of the bright, happy moon. The man who taught me love says, "You know, I have a new idea for our book." Music to my sensitive ears, even more beautiful than the pounding surf! Through the first six chapters, he called it "your book," and lo and behold—my dream come true! Back when I was a silly young girl—that lasted through the first half of my life—I used to daydream about having a husband with whom I could write a book. He doesn't want me to add his name to the title. Tomorrow we'll have a Fair Fight for Change about that. Oh, you want to know what his beach walk idea was? It was all about Sexuality, so we won't have the Fair Fight for Change tonight. Instead, "Honey, let's go home and practice for our Sexuality Chapter."

In our large bed with the romantic fragrance of intoxicating gardenias and exotic jasmine wafting through the windows into our special Garden of Delight, we remember our friends, the turtles, and we laugh as we lose track of who is leading and who is following, and who is touching and who is being touched, in this flowing above water dance of delight. Was that my hand touching your hand touching me? Legs wrapped around each other, long kisses that never quite end, and long, slow licks, squeezes, and feathery caresses. The end of one more perfect day of love in paradise.

"We shelter under a warm net of kisses. We drink from the well of each other's mouth."—Diane Ackerman

PASSENGER

I'm not here for me
I'm here for you.
When you go off like a rocket,
I want to go along for the ride.
—John Tyler

What a great way to have High Energy Fun and romance, feel cherished and totally relaxed, banish all thoughts and cares, and connect on a soul level with your Beloved! Sex isn't about physical gymnastics or techniques. You can read a hundred books with pictures explaining what to do. Forget all that, along with the messages you received growing up. We're not talking about sport sex or conquest sex, or relieving a sexual itch with a sneeze, or a step by step guide to a quick orgasm or relief. We're talking about something very different! Some call it Conscious Sex, Tantric Sex, Sacred Sex, High Sex, or Making Love. We call it Heaven on Earth.

A good sex life is the privilege and the heart of a good marriage, and the bedroom can be an oasis for light heartedness, laughter, adventure and a meeting of two souls.

SUNDAYS IN BED WITH YOU

Sunday morning in bed
eating croissants and drinking
hand squeezed orange juice
the New York Times on our bellies.

You reach for my hand
run your toes across my instep
tongue the special skin between
shoulder and nipple
squeeze the life into me
as I read about William Kennedy
in the Book Review.

I find it hard to concentrate
as I grow hard under your touch.
Parts of the paper
slide to the floor
as our bodies turn
into each other
and we make love.

The good news is all here
in our bedroom
some on the floor
more under the sheets
of news that cover our
gently heaving bodies
slowly cooling
in the fresh air
of another Sunday.
—John Tyler

One of the most creative and pleasurable tasks of marriage is to create a tender, passionate sexual relationship, and to guard it and nourish it so that it will endure. Sometimes one or both partners become bored with their marriage, because truly intimate eroticism and love without defensiveness are more threatening and fearful than they can tolerate. Finding the courage to risk opening to deep self-revealing sex and intimacy not only helps people grow up, it makes possible a profound and spiritual union with your beloved.

As Deepak Chopra says, in *The Path to Love*:

"What raises romantic love above lesser pleasures is that it stirs our deep erotic natures. This is yet another source of anxiety for modern people, who are obsessed by sex without being willing to lose control, without being able to surrender to real passion. Passion must contain surrender in order to be authentic. But surrender to what? To the convergence of all the aspects of your being that need to flow into the erotic moment. Physical sensuality, spiritual ecstasy, erotic flowering—when all of these converge, the sexual act becomes sacred, and what is sacred contains the deepest pleasure. Thousands of years ago, Lord Shiva murmured to his consort, 'While being caressed, sweet Princess, enter the caress as everlasting life.' This remains the ideal of intimacy."

If we didn't see our parents being affectionate with each other, or if we didn't experience closeness, warm touches, and unconditional love from them, or if we were rejected, ignored or hurt by a parent, we may be so afraid of disappointment or rejection or hurt that we hold back sexually. Unconsciously we know great sex would take our love to an unknown, unexplainable, unexplored and otherworldly dimension. *This fear of intimacy can be cured.* A good couple therapist specialist can help heal the wounds that interfere with the *great love life you deserve.*

The Japanese word for orgasm translates as "I have died and gone to heaven." Maybe that's one of the reasons why some people fear such a *complete* experience as the full body orgasm that happens in High Conscious

SEXUALITY & SENSUALITY OR MY SECRET FABULOUS LIFE IN PARADISE

Lovemaking. Often the belief system behind a couple's behavior creates a conflicted and unhappy relationship. As therapists, we like to challenge the interlocking assumptions and gender expectations that keep couples stuck.

Sexual energy is a bridge between the physical and the spiritual—that's why it's so powerful and full of ecstasy. Making love rejuvenates every cell in our body, and unites mind, body, heart and spirit in an explosive energy release. We need to transform our sex lives into a sacrament. God created sex—man screwed it up. In India, it is considered the most noble of the arts. Our goal is to make our sex life as conscious as the rest of our lives.

Doonesbury © G.B. Trudeau. Reprinted with permission of Universal Press Syndicate. All rights reserved.

We increase the energetic flow of passion and pleasure by making every touch a conscious touch, and we make our hands extensions of our hearts.

The communication, laughter, sensitivity, caring, tenderness, awareness, sensuality, sexuality and love that flow back and forth between you in the bedroom can be a metaphor for the rest of your relationship and the rest of your life. Transforming a good—or not so good—sexual relationship into conscious, sacred sex begins with how you treat each other all day long. Making love doesn't start late at night when you're so tired you decide to have quick sex so you can go to sleep. It's important to start the day with bonding, hugs, kisses, and sweet words. Continue with, perhaps, a noon "I love you" phone call, a love note in the bathroom or on the car windshield, a surprise in the lunch box, a hug and kiss at the end of the day, candles and flowers at dinner, careful listening, and nurturing support as the events of the day are shared. By the time you enter your Sacred Love Temple, you are feeling appreciated and cherished and longing for some good ole skin connection.

Now: Setting the Scene for your secret enchanted love life! First, make your bedroom a temple of love, with fragrant candles, romantic music, books of love poems, an erotic picture, and a big, comfortable bed. You might have a warming plate for massage oil, a feather, a mirror, and flowers. What do not belong are pictures of your parents, work papers, laundry, and any other clutter. Turn off the phone and the TV. Create a room for loving, for soft music, for reading good books, for inspiration, relaxing and sleeping. If you must talk about business, money, problems, or world famine and violence, gently take your partner's hand and lead her into the living room. Wise, conscious lovers keep their bedroom sanctuaries pure and free of negativity. You can feel the love energy as soon as you enter such an oasis.

SUGGESTIONS FOR CONSCIOUS LOVING

- Release anger daily. Forgive daily. *Never* take anger into the bedroom.
- Express love verbally and non-verbally every day.
- Perform Caring Behaviors daily.
- Create a peaceful, sacred, private love oasis in your bedroom, with candles, music, art, and poetry.
- Be relaxed and clean.
- Make time for sensual dates—morning, early afternoon, early evening—or make a date for the entire evening with child care provided for your children. Plan intimate dates, and also be sexually spontaneous when unplanned opportunities arise.
- Start and end each day with Bonding, so you start and end the day feeling loved.
- Encourage Free Child play: sex toys, use pet names, be silly, play fantasy games. Sex is not always serious—be as relaxed and childish and playful as you wish.
- Sleep nude. Muriel James says "You can make up for not getting enough touching in childhood by sleeping nude nightly with your partner."
- Let go of expectations of yourself and your partner. Forget simultaneous orgasm. *Forget orgasms!* As Deepak Chopra says in *The Path to Love*, "Orgasm is pursued with a devotion that would put most religious zealots to shame." Enjoy non-goal-oriented conscious loving without the expectation of orgasm. Let orgasms happen when they happen.
- Practice mutuality with both partners being honored and respected. Sometimes focus on giving one partner pleasure.
- Make noise. Breathe. Be yourself. Don't withhold. Surrender. Be adventurous and wild!
- Meditate on your partner. Be here now. Focus your full conscious attention on being present in each moment and movement of loving your partner.

- Don't fake orgasms. Any woman who fakes orgasm too often winds up not knowing whether she's coming or going.
- Sex is for love. Don't use it for manipulation, as a bargaining tool, or withhold it for revenge.
- *Blue Balls is a myth.* You *can* make love without sexual intercourse and without ejaculating.
- Talk about sex at times when you're not making love.
- Don't eat or drink too much.
- Trust and be vulnerable with each other. Learn what turns you on and what you need to be sexually aroused and satisfied, and in the appropriate manner and timing, share it with your partner. Teach your partner by showing her what you like, including masturbating. Be genuine and spontaneous in expressing your sexuality. Ask what turns her on and when you can, offer it. Don't make assumptions. Make it clear that you're hoping for the same honesty from her.
- Instead of thinking in terms of foreplay and afterglow, change your attitude—it's *all* making love. Be aware of the real pleasures of making love before and after sexual intercourse, and without sexual intercourse. Enjoy love for its own sake without focusing on performance, athleticism or orgasm.
- Be tender with each other. Become familiar with and enjoy your partner's entire body and her many, many erogenous zones. Don't fixate on genitals—her whole body craves touching: her face—a woman feels especially loved when her sweetheart caresses her face; her legs; her sweet behind; her hair. Love the other parts of her body for a long time before (or without) moving to her genitals. Our skin is our largest sensual and sexual organ of pleasure. Deepak Chopra says, "The human skin is the richest pharmacopoeia we have." Women, men have a variety of erogenous zones too—nipples, ears, testicles, and sweet behinds. Be gentle.
- Give up addictions, including workaholism, and nour-

ish your love by spending a great deal of time together.
- A woman's clitoris is the equivalent of a man's penis. Lovingly bestow the gift of an orgasm to her by gently caressing and licking her clitoris. Always take the time to arouse her in that way, *after* caressing her body all over, before entering her vagina.
- Non-orgasmic women and clitoris phobic men can be helped by psychotherapists specializing in couple or sex therapy.
- Slower. Gentler. Lighter. Longer. Easier. Softer. Slow. Slow. Slow.
- Make loving, gentle requests for change and *avoid criticism about anything, ever*. If you forget, be especially conscious *not* to criticize after 5:00 p.m.
- If you feel like making love and it doesn't happen that night, make it into "Ooops, no big deal!" instead of being a baby and acting like "I want what I want, and you have to give it to me right now!" Just snuggle up and go to sleep.
- Practice Tantra. Be conscious slow motion lovers in daily life—looking into each other's eyes, feeding, dancing, massaging, cooking, walking, listening, love talk, sensuous touch. Transcendental sex heals psycho-spiritual wounds, transforms relationships and is a spiritual path toward enlightenment.

Conscious lovers indulge in prolonged, lingering kisses, and keep their eyes open, while caressing their divine partner's adored body all over. Conscious lovers pay close attention to each other, stay in touch with each other's breathing, and talk and listen to each other on the most intimate personal level. They enjoy each other's smells, sounds and tastes. Oh! How good my dear, sweet O-o-o-o-z-y smells! I think his deep love and goodness ooze from the pores of his skin, and that's why he smells even better than all the pikake, tuberose, gardenias and jasmine in the garden outside our bedroom. Linger over your beloved's body, inhale deeply, savor the scent, explore different places on his body, and drink in the different tastes and fragrances. Find your favorite, most delectable spots on that receptive, precious body.

In addition to all this generic advice, you also need to find out the special things your unique partner likes. No matter how well you may have pleased your past practice lovers, that tells you nothing about your one and only now, with her own endearing idiosyncrasies. Find out by asking—ask at a time when you are *not* making love.

Make it easier and safer and more comfortable to talk about sex by lighting a candle, turning on soft music, facing each other, and agreeing to simply listen to what each has to say without judgment or defensiveness.

If a man's ego is all wrapped up in his penis, he thinks his power is wrapped up in his sexual performance. He may seem hurt and fragile if a woman asks for some things different from what he's been doing, or if she doesn't have an orgasm. Some women rescue their partners and pretend, adapt, don't say what they want, and fake orgasms. After faking so long, the act becomes louder and more exaggerated, and she loses touch with her real feelings, and finally she numbs completely. So we women need to have the courage to be authentic in our lovemaking if we want to introduce ourselves to the bliss of conscious love.

We each have a **P**arent, **A**dult and **C**hild inside of us. The Parent has two parts: the Critical Parent and the Nurturing Parent. The Critical Parent judges himself and others, and the Nurturing Parent cares for himself and others. The Child also has two distinct states: the Free Child, and the Adapted Child. The Adapted Child lives to please others, to be liked, or rebels from others to "show them". The Free Child has fun, expresses feelings, and is creative. All the healthy sexual energy comes from the Free Child.

SEXUALITY & SENSUALITY
OR MY SECRET FABULOUS LIFE IN PARADISE

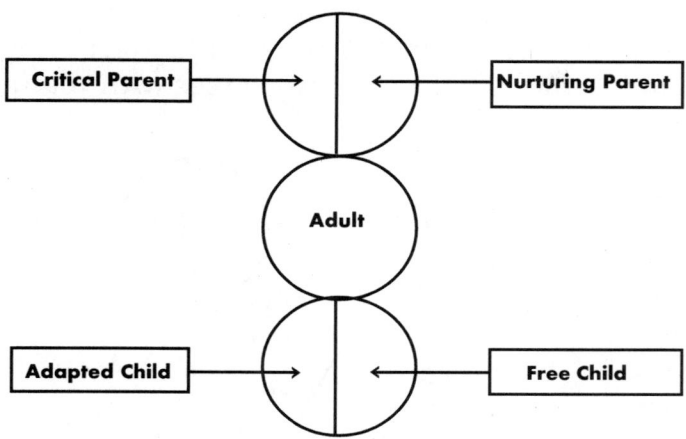

If you are adapted and pretending, just to please your partner, the Free Child cannot come out to play. The Adapted Child surrounds the Free Child, and when you're a people pleaser, even in love, your Free Child can hardly breathe, let alone know what she wants.

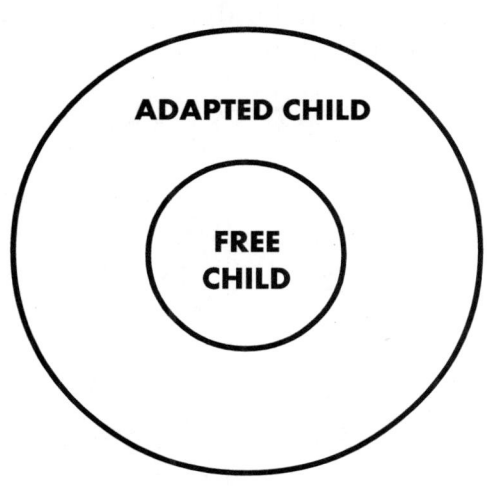

If you are in your Nurturing Parent Ego State to take care of your partner sexually, your Child won't meet with your lover's Child. It's no fun to have sex with your needy Child or with Mommy.

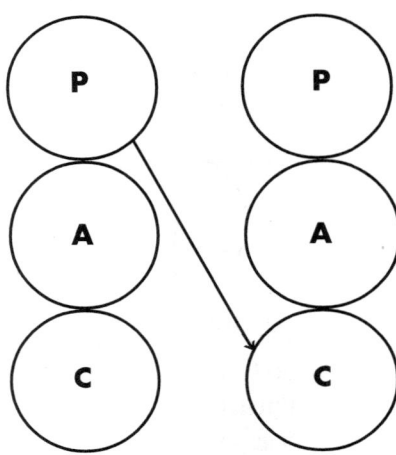

The next diagram demonstrates a symbiotic relationship, sometimes called "Codependent." One partner cathects the Parent and Adult ego states only, and the other is the needy Child. Not sexy ! ! !

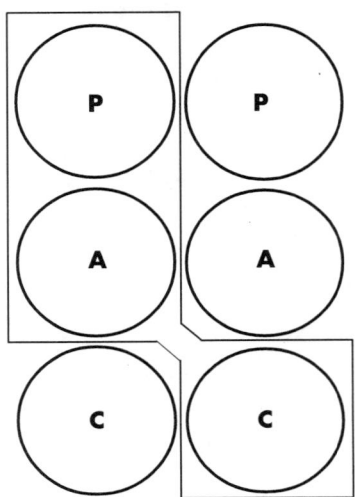

Great love relationships are between two healthy people with all three ego states intact, the Adult in the executive role and in charge of letting the Free Child come out to play when it's lovemaking playtime! We are all entitled to pleasure, happiness and bliss. Pleasure is feeling good, having fun, and enjoying activities. Happiness is feeling safety and passion in life; putting ourselves in safe situations with safe people, especially in our primary relationship; and letting go of control and surrendering to equality with our partner. Bliss is feeling happy for no reason whatsoever.

The largest instrument of sex is not between the legs, it is between the ears—your mind. What goes on in your head will determine your sexual responsiveness. The largest body area for receiving sexual pleasure is the skin, and the chief instruments for giving pleasure are the hands and mouth.

For women, sexuality and spirituality are linked at the source. Deep sexual satisfaction is more than just physical release, it's a sense of oneness with Spirit. It can create new pathways in the brain powerful enough to heal histories of sexual abuse.

Tantric sex is a slow motion dedication to each other, connecting bodies, hearts, minds and souls. For men, introducing Tantra into your sexual relationship with your lover can bring you to new heights of sexual competence, full of tenderness, awareness, spirituality, completion and love.

Tantra is a complex collection of Hindu and Buddhist texts and practices dating back to the sixth century A. D. Tantric teachings are nondogmatic and offer no clear record of their origins, even when it comes to the derivation of the Sanskrit term *tantra*: It is variously defined as meaning "web," "weaving," "expansion," and "liberation."

The idea that sex isn't good unless one or both partners come, and especially that both partners come at the same time, is an old wives (and husband's) tale. You can have an orgasm and lousy sex, and you can have incredible sex without an orgasm. Tantra teaches us to experience new heights of sexual and sensual ecstasy without ejaculation.

Once we learn some of the simplest ways to control ejaculation and orgasm, we enhance our mutual pleasure enormously. When we can exercise this degree of control over our sexuality, we become more confident about sex, and this enables us to truly relax and enjoy the ride! Then we can fully accept the idea that orgasm sometimes happens in the middle of making love, and sometimes doesn't happen, and loving is just as wonderful both ways. Conscious, sacred sex is not focused on orgasm, but on total bodily pleasure.

Some people place undue emphasis on sexual technique—athletic prowess in bed, or the number of orgasms. Making love is not a performance. This is a sign of too much focus on the genitals, too much emphasis placed on the outcome, and not enough attention devoted to enjoying each other and pleasuring each other in the moment.

Margo Anand says in *The Art of Sexual Magic*: "Sexual magic works on the spiritual level to heal wounds and connect you with spirit and the universe. And because it's sex, it also works on the physical level. When you practice sexual magic, you learn to give and receive such great pleasure that orgasm can be extended for hours."

Here are some of the most important concepts in Tantra:
• Your love, harmony and connection as a couple are part of your spiritual path.
• SLOW DOWN. Your sexual loving is a meditation.
• Remember that conscious loving is an art—you'll get better with time and practice.

SEXUALITY & SENSUALITY
OR MY SECRET FABULOUS LIFE IN PARADISE

- Speak to one another consciously, without criticism or blame.
- Be aware of your hands when you touch. Imagine your are sending energy from your heart and soul through your fingers into your beloved's body. Make every touch a conscious touch.
- Your body is the temple of your spirit. Treat your temple and your Beloved's well.
- If one of you is too tired or "stuck" to nurture the other, do it anyway. Making the effort will help you feel less tired and stuck.
- Keep your eyes open to stay in touch with your partner during love in this intimate way.

Tantric lovers sometimes start their day as a meditation with the Daily Devotion Tantric ritual. Upon awakening, they bond for several minutes. Then the man gently lubricates the woman's vagina and carefully places his penis inside her. They lie together like this without any movement for several minutes, breathing in unison and looking deep into each other's eyes. They focus on the flow of love between them, without any sense of sexual arousal. The sexual energy they generate is retained inside their bodies, providing them with wonderful loving energy to start the day together.

In the evening a suggested meditation to end the day before entering the marriage bed is the Melting Hug and Heart Salutation. In this practice, stand facing each other across the bedroom. Walk slowly towards each other, looking into each other's eyes, and embrace in a Melting Hug, in which you hold each other, touching from knees to cheeks, breathing gently in unison. Then move about 18 inches apart, still looking into each other's eyes. The man says, "I honor the Shakhti in you," and the woman says, "I honor the Shiva in you." Both bow from the waist until your foreheads gently touch, and breathing together, continue touching foreheads for a minute or two. Then straighten and slowly sink to the floor, sitting cross legged facing each other. Place your right hand on your partner's heart and your left hand over your partner's hand on your heart, look into each other's eyes and repeat: "I honor you as an aspect of myself. I honor the divine spirit in you."

These rituals transform sex into a loving prayer, and bring us into an experience of oneness. Each of us has the potential to be spontaneous—to find our freedom within—and this can be cultivated and cherished by creative couples. One of our clients told us that he and his wife had lived with her parents until they had children. Then they lived in crowded city apartments. It wasn't until the children moved out that he discovered new facets to their lovemaking. On the second night that they were completely alone, his wife began making loud, pleasurable noises during intercourse until she was shouting when she reached orgasm. This turned him on so much that he immediately climaxed. Discussing it afterwards, she said that she always had an urge to give full voice to her ardent excitement, but she was inhibited, first by the proximity of her parents in their house, and then by the nearness of their children. Thus their sexual sounds were limited to murmurs. Now they enjoy chasing each other through the house with shouts of joy and merriment. They enhance their love play with laughter and all the other erotic sounds that signify pleasure.

Conversely, another couple told us that they have their best sex when they stay overnight at her parent's home. Unlike their usual routine, they stay up half the night making love. They couldn't understand it until one night, when they had gone to bed first, they heard her parents coming upstairs. Simultaneously they realized what a turn-on it was—feeling like 'bad" children. But it was so much fun they saw no reason to stop. Her parents are pleased with their frequent overnight visits, and they are too.

Other couples use terms of endearment or words of

SEXUALITY & SENSUALITY OR MY SECRET FABULOUS LIFE IN PARADISE

praise for their partner, which spur each to greater heights. Even the one word, "Yes!" said over and over with increasing intensity is stimulating. Some couples enjoy going to bed with sexy books or magazines to read aloud to each other while quietly becoming more aroused. This talking to heighten lust is called "ecouterism," from the French word "ecouter," to listen.

©Peter Mueller, Reprinted with Permission

Let's talk about fantasies. Talk to your lover about all those hot and sultry places your fantasies have taken you. Whisper those thoughts to each other as you begin to make love. Share them in the heat of passion. Don't be shy. Give details. Say things you've never said before. When he shares his fantasies, listen to your lover and really hear what he is saying. His sensual or wicked fantasies can either wash over you like a warm waterfall, or plunge you into an earthquake of excitement, or both. Sexual fantasies can be great adventures.

©John Grimes, Reprinted with Permission

It's time to leap over those barriers of inhibition that have been keeping you from experiencing all the "forbidden" pleasure you and your partner deserve. Go ahead! Take the risk! Be spontaneous. Whatever pops into your head—whatever wild, zany thing you want to try in the bedroom—go ahead! Once you've tried it, you'll never forget the sheer Free Child pleasure of being spontaneous with your beloved. And be sure to keep your lover guessing! He'll love a bit of mystery, a bit of intrigue, that hint of uncertainty that adds spice to your love life. Deepak Chopra says, "The higher the level of unpredictability, the higher the awareness."

One of our darling happy, healthy client couples shared with us the richness of their sex life. In the midst of their lovemaking, Marc was astonished to hear Betsy suddenly say, "Hurry, my husband's coming!" Marc found it both funny and wonderful at the same time. Since then he occasionally plays the role of a sympathetic, exciting secret lover while she is the naughty, sneaky seductress she always wanted to be.

Sometimes the Greatest Lover of All Time will start talking to me in a foreign accent, or I'll do my Southern Belle number. He might enter our oasis of love and say, "What are you doing in my hotel room?" I'll say, "This is my room! The clerk told me it was the last room in the hotel." Then we'll work it out so this complete stranger and I spend the night together based on his promise to stay on his side of the bed, which of course he manages to forget in deliciously wicked ways!

Sometimes we are teenage sweethearts in my bedroom afraid my parents will come home and catch us. Create your own play, reinvent yourselves, and have so much fun acting out your roles that you forget who you are. We all consist of many parts, and that fantasy might touch on one of your parts and let you become someone you've always wanted to be. Enjoy being different, and being with that other fascinating person in your own lover's body. Sometimes we even forget we're not teenagers, and I do believe we regress and grow younger each time we play teenagers making love!

As teenagers in our 60's and beyond, growing older and younger together we feel younger and healthier, and we have more wonderful sex with each other with each too quickly passing year! When we have sexual thoughts or fantasies, our body systems work better, aging effects are diminished, and we stay young. However, if we allow criticism or guilt or loneliness to mix with the play of healthy sexual thought, these beneficial effects are lost.

Many women find middle age a time of sexual liberation. After years of feeling inhibited—often due to the time constraints and emotional demands of child rearing—middle aged women begin to seek greater satisfaction from lovemaking. They become more comfortable with their bodies, and they are more open to experimentation and more willing to experience and enjoy the richness of conscious lovemaking.

The Golden Years can be the most peaceful and adventurous period in your sexual life. After you've raised your children is an ideal time to begin. Some couples tell us that they felt safe to open themselves up to Conscious Love after the nest was empty, and before it filled up again with grandchildren. Your Golden Years are a great time to start this magical practice.

For men over 65 or 70, remember, just because your legs aren't as strong as they were when you were twenty, you don't have to give up walking or running. You may walk a little slower and run a little less, but you still get where you are going. Well, the same is true of sex. Why should you feel, because your sexual "muscles" are not as strong as they once were, that you will stop having sex? On the contrary, some changes that come with maturity may actually help you be an even better lover. These physiological changes are different for each person, and happen any time between age 50 and age 80. First, you may become slower to have a spontaneous erection, although this is not true for every man. You may need more direct physical stimulation from your partner, using her hands, her mouth, and her breasts to stimulate your penis. This can provide a most pleasurable addition to your lovemaking, and can give her pride in her skill as a sexual partner and in her ability to turn you on. Remember, this doesn't mean you won't get hard or be able to make love—only that you need your partner's help. If you are upset or worried, that will interfere more with your ability to be relaxed and centered in your lovemaking than any physiological changes. Another important point is that, even though your erection may not be as hard and firm or last as long as it did in your twenties, you can still be a great lover by concentrating on your lover and pleasing her with your hands and tongue.

Shere Hite says, in *The Hite Report on Male Sexuality*, "Older men, who *may* have trouble achieving or maintaining an erection, have been ridiculed and made to feel 'less than' by the society. In fact, often their diversification and rethinking of sexual pleasure have made them better lovers than younger men."

Another area of concern is wanting sex less often. Men over sixty or seventy are often satisfied with one or two climaxes per week. This does not mean that you will only desire or be able to have sex once or twice a week. You can make love much more frequently, but you do not need or desire an orgasm every time. Some men believe they are failing their partners unless they climax every time. If you try to force an erection, you will surely lose it. When you notice that you are having sex but not needing to come every time, it is an opportunity to become a better, more patient lover. You may be able to maintain your erection for a longer time without climaxing. Most women appreciate a man who takes a long time to make love. Your mental attitude about the changes you experience as you grow older is more important than the effect those changes may have on your body. If you see these changes as providing an opportunity to become a better lover, you will welcome the changes and incorporate them into your love life.

While going through his father's bureau after he died at age 79, my sentimental husband found this article from *Trade Magazine*, November 30, 1981: "Want to stay sharp? Preserve your memory? Then maintain an active sex life through your old age. These are the words of wisdom from Dr. Lars Nilsson, whose research team did a long-term study of a group of persons over 70 in Goteborg, Sweden. 'To give up one's sexual life leads to a drop in memory capacity and intellectual ability,' says Dr. Nilsson."

We know women and men in their 80's who still have tender and passionate sex. Keep practicing, and bringing surprises and romance into each other's lives. We *can* keep riding the wave of bliss through our *glorious* Golden Years.

We need to be playful and release our wild energy for sexual healing. So yell, scream, growl, bite gently, pretend you're jungle animals, have a rollicking good time. If the kids ask what the commotion was all about, tell them the truth: "We were being wild and silly and playing games and having fun in bed because we love each other so much." How happy and healthy it is for children to know their parents play too, and that they love each other!

Sex is only healthy and all it can be in equal relationships. People who have either conscious or unconscious deep fears of intimacy, or who don't have enough healthy excitement in their lives, create drama by becoming a Rescuer, a Persecutor, or a Victim as a way of keeping negative excitement while avoiding intimacy.

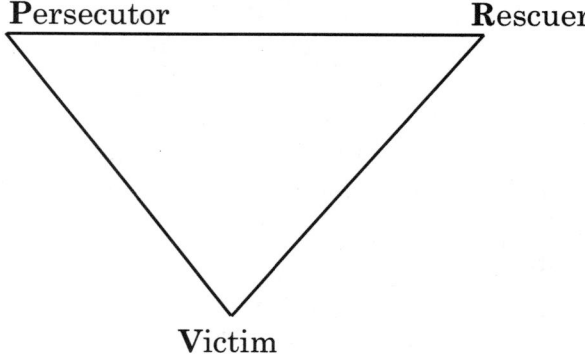

The Drama Triangle is explained in Chapter 2.

SEXUALITY & SENSUALITY
OR MY SECRET FABULOUS LIFE IN PARADISE

Don't Rescue your partner and "perform" sex because he "needs it," or Persecute your spouse with violent passion to make up, and don't be a Victim and allow sexual practices you find abhorrent, or allow yourself to be used for sex without love.

Healthy sex and love flow between the Child Ego States in both partners, not between a parent and child or two adults having sex from their heads with memorized routines. Sex, creativity, and spirituality all come from the Child Ego State.

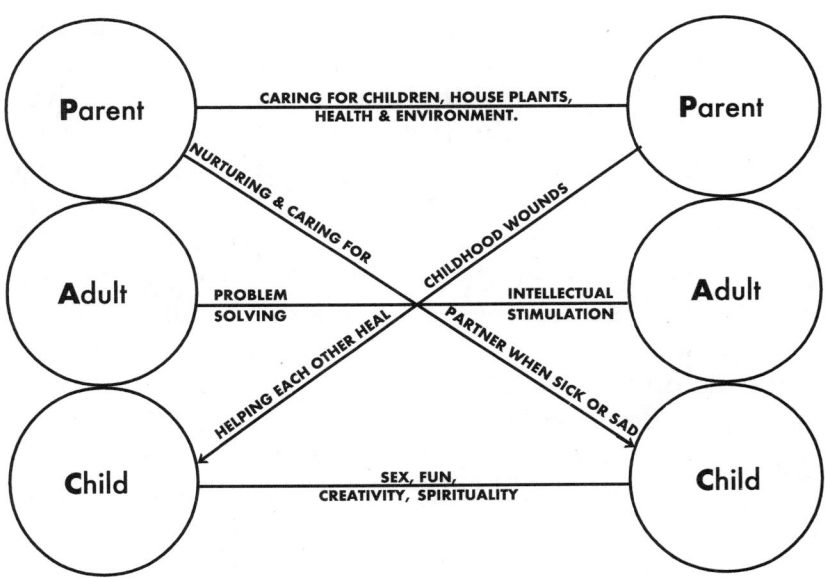

When we Conscious Lovers kiss, we taste each other's essence for long periods of time. We first receive each other's mouths, and then explore other delectable places. Kissing affects secretion, and we give and receive through kissing. Sexual loving has a limitless menu, and yet it's important to choose only comfortable positions. Loving is easy, not hard work. We need to let our innermost self come out to play with our sweetheart, our open eyes looking deep into her soul. It never hurts to open, but it hurts to close down and go numb. Some boys learn at 14 or 15 or 16 to get it up, get it in, and get it off. Well, as comedian Joan Rivers would say, "Grow up!" We need to transform the quick fix sneeze genital ejaculation into full-body, tingling-all-over ecstasy, when the mind stops and we disappear into each other. We need to quiet the mind that remembers techniques, other women, and what needs to happen at work tomorrow. Only the right, creative side of the brain is invited to the love bed, along with the body, heart and soul. This isn't about technique, but about higher consciousness. This is more than sex—it's healing, freeing great amounts of creative energy, focusing 100% of your attention on your dearest darling, as in a deep, life-enhancing meditation, empowering each other in a mutual Higher Self connection to spirit, regenerating every cell in your bodies, and facilitating a Higher Consciousness.

I have read that 50% of American women are non-orgasmic. In some cases, women have been stifled and disempowered by men. In worse cases, they've been used, bruised and abused. What a great opportunity for a man to be a healer hero by providing the safety the woman needs in order to feel and express the full amount of passion that is her true nature. All of this hinges on your ability to be slow, soft—yes, I said soft!—to use all your senses: see her fully, touch her gently, taste and smell her deliciousness, speak to her in compliments, appreciations, songs, poetry, private love names, and questions like "What would you like me to do?" and—surprise!—most important—*open your ears* and *listen* to her. She craves being *really* heard—not in passing, perhaps the way her parents did, but truly concentrating on her words. This is what sustains the safety and passion in a long term committed relationship—talking and listening to each other on the most intimate personal level. Pay attention to the most important person in your life.

SEXUALITY & SENSUALITY OR MY SECRET FABULOUS LIFE IN PARADISE

SEXUAL ASSERTIVENESS AFFIRMATIONS

Here are some Sexual Assertiveness Affirmations. Find which ones you *need*, choose several, and say them to yourself in a loving voice morning and night looking into your eyes in the mirror every day for 21 *consecutive* days. That's how long self-hypnosis takes. If you miss a day, start all over again.

• I, (name), can easily tell my partner what feels good, and I communicate my sexual wishes easily.
• It is okay to communicate my sexual needs to [partner's name]. It is good to say "I want."
• Whenever I, (name), hesitate in the verbalization of my sexual feelings, I will probe deeper.
• I, (name), am comfortable asking for information about sex.
• I, (name), am able to put my feelings into words.
• I, (name), have the right to say no without losing my partner's love.
• I, (name), acknowledge my partner verbally whenever I like what is being done.
• I, (name), am secure enough to admit it when I feel vulnerable and need love.
• I, (name), get rewarded for revealing my feelings.
• I, (name), look at what thoughts are going on within me without judgment or blame.
• I, (name), have a right to express my true feelings wherever I am, no matter who I am with.
• I, (name), deserve all the time and attention I need, and I ask for what I want.
• I, (name), can relax and enjoy myself, and please my partner later.
• When it is my turn to receive, it is perfectly okay to concentrate totally on myself.

WHEN ONE PARTNER WANTS SEX MORE THAN THE OTHER

To achieve true sexual intimacy, we need to let go of hierarchy in our sexual relationships. The person with the lower sexual desire controls sex. We need to meet somewhere in between, instead of controlling the amount of sexual activity through game playing, manipulation or power plays. If your partner has a lower desire than you do, become an expert in creating desire in your partner. Define the conditions that make you most eager for lovemaking, and let your partner know about them. Be willing to meet each other's sexual preconditions, those qualities that enhance your willingness to make love. Don't expect your partner to do all the work. Let your partner know what turns you on. And finally, when you don't feel like making love, say so—and don't feel guilty. If you make an effort to meet your partner's sexual needs much of the time, you don't have to feel guilty those times you say no. But when you say no, also say when. In other words, let your partner know when you will be available.

CONSCIOUS SENSUAL DATE

Couples who have been having sexual intercourse for a while frequently report that sex has become quite routine. The emphasis is on intercourse itself and quick sexual release. Often, the couple will recall their first sexual experiences, and long for those remembered feelings of excitement, spontaneity, and seductive touching. That narrow focus on intercourse has blinded them to the pleasurable touching, the feelings of sensuality, and the true breadth and depth of their sexuality. The fun and spontaneity have gone out of sex and been replaced by a rigid goal orientation focused on orgasm.

If this has happened to you, you need to shift your focus away from genital orgasm and reorient your attitudes and feelings toward more slow, sensual pleasuring. One way to do this is to plan a purely sensual pleasure date. Create a time and place that gives you the privacy and safety you both need to feel comfortable exploring and discovering sensual pleasure. *Mutually agree that the session will not progress to sexual intercourse.*

Allow yourselves full range to discover the pleasure you can derive simply from touching and being touched. Take the time to explore what style of touching, stroking and caressing feels most pleasurable and enjoyable. Concentrate on pleasure and communicating what gives you each pleasure. Take turns, with one of you totally focused on pleasuring the other, and the receiver totally focused on learning what feels pleasurable and communicating this to the giver.

As the giver, make a point of touching your partner in the ways and with the pressure she tells you she likes. Ask for her help if you don't understand, even to the point of letting her guide your hands so you can learn just the way and manner that feels most pleasing to her.

This exercise helps you both become comfortable with touching, discovering and sharing what pleases each of you, with a minimum of attention on performance. Then you can use this information in your sexual lovemaking to enhance the pleasure for both partners.

CONSCIOUS SEXUAL DATE

Here is a special date you might plan with pleasure and love each week or each month:

6:00 MEET—Shower, change, Melting Hug described on page 157.
6:30 CONNECT—In any of the following ways: lie in a hot tub, walk in woods, watch the sunset, read poetry or erotic literature aloud to each other, move loving energy between you with kisses, listen to music, look at erotic

art, feed each other finger food or a light dinner.
7:30 BOND—More long, juicy, drawn-out kisses, Heart Salutation described on page 157.
Talk about vision, dreams, good memories, share ideas, feelings, with candles, music, aroma of fresh flowers. Lovingly caress face and hair.
8:00 TOUCH—Caressing and teasing session with feathers, erotic dance, pet names, appreciations, strokes, love words, more kisses, massage, continue music and candles.
8:30 PLEASURING—Share fantasies, show what you like and how you like it, kisses, more caresses, laughter, moans, more appreciations, play, love sounds. Use the information you learned in the Conscious Sensual Date to pleasure each other.
9:00 ECSTATIC BLISS—Touch each other all over, many kisses, love words, take all the time you need for many little orgasms or full body orgasm.
9:45 CELEBRATION—Chocolate and cognac, love talk, pet names, appreciations, kisses, sweet caresses, bonding, share sleepy time tape, blow out candles, express gratitude for this day and night.
10:15 SLEEP.

Remember: keep your activities and time flexible, and adapt to any spontaneous changes in mood that occur during your session. If you have young children, a baby sitter is the answer. If that's not possible, begin the evening later, after they are all in bed. If there are teenagers, tell them this is your private date—good role modeling—and ask them to respect your privacy. Change the hours according to your work and parenting duties. Some couples commit to one night together every week—one week out to dinner and a movie, concert or dancing, and the next week an evening for love and intimacy.

SOME REMARKABLE THINGS I KNOW THAT I'M FINALLY TELLING

by
John Tyler

- Conscious Loving is for healing and joining. Be aware of what pleases your partner and consciously offer what she likes.
- Your penis is a transmitter and receiver of the highest energy. Allow yourself to feel yourself giving and receiving love with and through your penis. Use your penis as a loving wand of pleasure, not a thrusting, masturbation device that desensitizes your partner. Use it to exchange energy in love, not to relieve tension.
- Open the fragile gates of your woman's enchanted garden with your delicate paint brushes—your fingers, tongue and eyes.
- You are there to heal, cherish, and embrace the Goddess, and to introduce her to Heaven, not to get off on her.
- Your desired one will be more available to you if you are open-hearted, attentive, conscious, and take *all the time she needs.*

"If we had over the moon sex on a regular basis, sex that rings from the soul and sends shock waves through us, there would be less disease, less anger, less war. If every man and woman alive could feel the crazy, delirious rush of the soul when it touches the soul of another, this world would be a happier place."
—Marianne Williamson

SHADOWS & LIGHT

The curved shadow of your breast
falls on your thigh
as you bend over me
flooding me with your love.

The oil lamp flickers and flicks
its light on your back,
mirrors your motion,
a soundless rhythm
to music we both can hear.

The lamp feeds the shadow,
needs the shadow
to mirror its purpose and beauty,
as I need you to show me mine.
—John Tyler

Hey, happy campers, this strangely turned into one of the longest chapters in the book, which reflects my views on the importance we ought to give sex in our lives. I hope you enjoyed lingering without being rushed. People don't usually save enough time for sex. Conscious lovers do. Conscious non-goal-oriented, slow motion sex is emotional starlight and deep powerful healing.

"God created the universe to have fun."—Deepak Chopra

—Notes—

—Notes—

9
Keeping the Spark Alive

"Love is like the moon. When it does not increase it decreases."
—Segur

We need to keep the candle lit or it will go out. Guess what!!! People do not just get married and live happily every after. Just as with any great work, there is more to it than "I do." I invite you to tape the following guided imagery and listen to it together with your eyes closed, or read it to each other—one relaxes with closed eyes and gentle flute or other meditative music while the other reads, and then you reverse roles:

THE SECRET GARDEN*

You're taking a walk on the grounds of a large estate. You see a high stone wall that is practically obscured with ivy. In the wall you notice a wooden door. On impulse you push open the wooden door and step through. You realize that you are inside an old walled garden. It's a garden that must once have been a lovely, formal garden, but no one has been tending it. The plants are so overgrown and there are so many weeds that it's hard to tell which are paths and which are garden plots. Starting in one part of the garden, see yourself pruning, weeding, mowing, cultivating, transplanting, watering and doing whatever needs to be done to put the garden back in order again...If you need any encouragement, stand back and

*Adapted with my additions from A Guided Imagery by Janette Rainwater

compare the part of the garden you have been working on with the part that you haven't touched.

    This is a metaphor for your relationship. Your relationship garden also needs regular attention: fertilizing with candles, flowers and music; nourishing with words of love; nurturing with caring behaviors; cultivating with high-energy fun; transplanting with surprises; and watering with daily sprinkles of romance.
    Albert Einstein said, "Imagination is more important than knowledge," and we need to use our imagination to generate excitement by planning small romantic trysts, unexpected surprises, wild adventures and hilarious moments.
    Love ebbs and flows, and the spark can stay lit if we both bring Aliveness to the relationship by being fascinating people who are fascinated with the otherness of our life companion. I am often surprised by things my husband of many years says to people, including me. The other day he said to me, "I didn't know you wrote greeting cards!" when he found the file in a drawer. We are constantly surprised and delighted by unusual discoveries. Here are some things you can do to bring vitality to your relationship. Don't give any hints or warnings to your partner—just do it!

- Cut your hair differently.
- Write a poem or love note and put it on her pillow, under the windshield wiper of her car, or some other surprising place.
- Read a poem aloud by candlelight.
- Sing to your lover while driving.
- Hire a sky writer to say "I love you Susan" (unless that is not her name!!).
- Send flowers to the office.
- Bring a dozen colored balloons "to celebrate my love for you".
- Hold hands while taking a moonlit walk.

KEEPING THE SPARK ALIVE

- Bring her bubble bath and run it in hot water for her relaxation.
- Watch the sun set in each other's arms.
- Stay in bed until noon calling each other silly love names.
- Compliment her in public.
- Wear something different from anything you have ever worn before and walk with a different gait—maybe a stride or a slink!
- Seduce him slowly.
- Talk in an accent or use a foreign expression.
- Cook for and feed the homeless together one night a week, and then take a walk by the light of the moon or go sit in front of the fireplace, and tell each other all the things in your life for which you are grateful.

Dear lighters of the Spark, I suggest you start with some of my ideas and allow them to inspire you onward with some wacky, radical, or just plain sweet ideas of your own!

The Australian writer, Bryce Courtney, said in his closing night speech at the Maui Writers Conference, "I was skating on thin ice, so I decided to tap dance." If your relationship is on thin ice, instead of freezing in fear or skating away scared, have some fun with your own original life-affirming dance, and you are likely to keep it a two step and firm up the ice at the same time.

Variety is the spice of life. Go on adventures together and take turns planning them—a hike, a walk in an unfamiliar neighborhood; inviting new friends for dinner; dining at a Vietnamese restaurant; or just saying positive things about every person, place and experience you know or have ever heard about for a whole weekend. Henry David Thoreau said, "The effect of the quality of the day—that is the highest of the arts."

During one of our PAIRS® groups Margy said, "I don't know if Rick loves me or not." I said, "Ask him!" Before she could get the words out of her mouth, he said,

"You shouldn't have to ask—I married you, didn't I?" Joan chimed in with, "When I ask Eric that question, he says, "Come to bed and I'll prove that I do." Wrong answers! ! ! The answer is "Yes, I love you," said with feeling while looking into your partner's eyes. "I love you." Learn it in a few other languages too, and say it spontaneously, often—without being asked. When you awaken in the morning start your day with, "I love you." Greet each other at dinnertime with, "I love you." When you are dining at a restaurant, or during commercials on television, and you are too tired to talk, just say, "I love you." That is worth a million other words. And please let "I love you" be your last words to each other before you fall asleep at night.

Perhaps it seems to some of you gentle readers that it's easier to keep the spark alive here on our Pacific island than where you are in New York City, or Iowa, or Cincinnati. There are couples on Maui who both work two or three jobs to be able to afford to live in the state with the highest cost of living. There are people here who are single and lonely, and people everywhere, even here, who have decided to stay stuck in the past, to withhold forgiveness, and to forego the spark of an exhilarating life. It doesn't matter where you live. Life is decisional, and you decide where to be, with whom to be in relationship, and what to do with your days.

Most of our friends in our age group are retired. We choose to live on Maui and keep working and being happy and in love, even when we have concerns about our children, grandchildren, and bank account, and even when our working hours seem long. We see couples at night while some people watch the wasteland of television. We swim in the mornings, while some go to their 8-6 jobs. We create our spark and we keep it lit, and you can too, wherever you have chosen to live. A healthy partnership is when two people have a mutual, contagious, vital potential for mutual cherishing.

PALAUEA BEACH

The sky is blue without a cloud
The sun is warm. The breeze is cool
We swim and play with graceful turtles
and eat our lunch in silent peace.

You made those huge sandwiches so juicy
So much like the way you make love.
We watch a breaching whale—
    the perfect day.
You look at me intently and say
"I love you more than yesterday."

I say, "I love you more than this
    morning!"
We look into each other's eyes—
there's nowhere else we'd rather be.
                      —Natalie Tyler

"Come and see my shining palace built upon the sand."—Edna St. Vincent Millay

—Notes—

10
Forgiveness

"Forgiveness is what you do with what's been done to you."
—Jean Paul Sartre

"Forgiveness is still, and quietly does nothing. It offends no aspect of reality, nor seeks to twist it to appearances it likes. It merely looks, and waits, and judges not."[1]—A Course in Miracles

The same qualities that go to make up a fulfilling relationship—love, commitment, forgiveness, surrender and honesty—are also the qualities that contribute to our spiritual growth. I learned the importance of daily forgiveness a long time ago at a week long spiritual Sufi retreat at Omega Institute in Rhinebeck, New York, when Rabbi Zalman Shalomi-Schachter taught us this ritual. I highly recommend it to all of you. At the end of each day before you go to bed, light two candles—candles soften the atmosphere—and each of you say, "I'm sorry for anything I may have done that hurt you today, and I forgive you for anything you may have done or refrained from doing that hurt me." Then you blow out each other's candle and go to sleep in peace and have sweet dreams. As A Course In Miracles says, "All forgiveness is a gift to yourself."[2]

"What does it mean to forgive?" asked Elsie, who is still so mad at her father and her first husband that her anger sometimes leaks out at Chuck, her easy-going present husband. To forgive, according to Webster's dictionary, means:
• To let go of, or give up resentment against, or grievances held against;
• To let go of or give up the desire to attack, punish, or get back at.
• To stop being angry at, annoyed or irritated with.
• To give up all claim to punish or exact penalty for (an offense); to overlook.

Dag Hammarskjold, the former Secretary General of the United Nations, said, "Forgiveness is the answer to the child's dream of a miracle by which what is broken is made whole again. What is soiled is made clean." In

FORGIVENESS

Heart Empowerment, Doc Lew Childre teaches that "Forgiveness is a power tool for releasing judgment, resentment or other negative emotional reactions that produce stress in your system."

Former Assistant Secretary General of the United Nations, Robert Muller, wrote these beautiful lines in 1992 in observance of International Forgiveness Week February 16 through February 22:

DECIDE TO FORGIVE

Decide to forgive
For resentment is negative
Resentment is poisonous
Resentment diminishes
and devours the self.

Be the first to forgive,
To smile and to take the first step,
And you will see happiness bloom
On the face of your human brother or sister.

Be always the first
Do not wait for others to forgive
For by forgiving
You become the master of fate,
The fashioner of life,
The doer of miracles.

To forgive is the highest,
Most beautiful form of love.
In return you will receive
Untold peace and happiness.

He continued with his "program for achieving a truly forgiving heart:
- Sunday: Forgive yourself.
- Monday: Forgive your family.
- Tuesday: Forgive your friends and associates.
- Wednesday: Forgive across economic lines within your own nation.
- Thursday: Forgive across cultural lines within your own nation.
- Friday: Forgive across political lines within your own nation.
- Saturday: Forgive other nations."

Mahatma Gandhi said, "Only the brave know how to forgive. A coward never forgives. It is not in his nature."

The first step toward living a life of forgiveness is to forgive yourself. Pir Vilayat Inayat Kahn has said in his wise writings:

"There's no way of documenting this, but we know that every fragment of the universe is linked with every other. Whatever happens—one wave rises in the Atlantic, and the whole Pacific Ocean has to adapt—everything is interrelated. That's a very important thought, because we have difficulty in forgiving ourselves, and think that the past is the past and there is nothing we can do to change it. The fact is that the past is in some way changed in the present; it is no more what it was. As much as we change the present we are also retroactively changing the past. It's a difficult thought; we're not used to thinking that way." A Course In Miracles says, "Unless the past is over in my mind, the real world must escape my sight."[3]

Forgiving ourselves is much harder than forgiving others, so we carry a burden of guilt over our mistakes. We need forgiveness to acknowledge our mistakes and learn from them, and then forgive ourselves, forget and move on. What we did in the past was the best we could

FORGIVENESS

do with what we knew at the time, with the resources we had then, considering where we were developmentally, our unhealed soul wounds, and who we were before the experiences, the knowledge, the wisdom and the love we have accumulated over the years.

Every human being, at every moment of the past—when the entire situation is taken into account—has done the very best he could do under the circumstances, and so deserves neither blame nor reproach from anyone—including himself. This is particularly true of each of you. Your cells are constantly being regenerated. We replace every cell in our bodies every seven years, so you are not the same person you were seven years ago. Your mother and father are not the same people they were when you were a child. Perhaps their parenting was flawed by the hardship, trouble, sickness, insanity or lovelessness they were tortured by, which you could not have known about. We must be able to forgive ourselves in order to forgive others, and we cannot forgive ourselves until we are willing to forgive others. Ultimately on a spiritual level, we are all one.

We reinvent ourselves and our lives many times as we mature. If we did not we would be grown up bodies stuck in teenage rebellion or three year-old thinking processes. Sometimes I think of that woman—now she seems like a girl—named Natalie at age twenty-one, and even at age forty-one, and how little she knew and how unaware she was about her values and her true identity. And yet she thought she knew it all, and I marvel at how much more I have to learn, and how every day I learn something new. When we think we know it all about any person or any concept, place or subject, we haven't learned many lessons, and we can be certain there's a great deal we have to learn. When ghosts from the past visit, they want to be taken into your silent place and be healed by you.

The highest place we can go in our spiritual development is to forgive ourselves and all others. A Course in Miracles says, "The holiest place of all the spots on earth is where an ancient hatred has become a present love."[4] We must forgive ourselves, our parents, and our real and imagined enemies to be able to forgive our present spouse, our children, and all those close to us for their daily mistakes and imperfections. A Course In Miracles says, "Do you prefer that you be right or happy?"[5] If you want to be the loving, gentle, kind, content, at-peace person you are becoming, then your partner is your opportunity. If you truly want to learn forgiveness, then with whom can you practice each day and forgive more fully than your partner? A Course in Miracles says, "The one wholly true thought about the past is that it is not here."[6]

Unchain yourself from the past

Reprinted with Permission

FORGIVENESS

We have all been hurt. It is what we do with our hurt that makes the difference in our lives. Past losses and unresolved issues impact our present day relationships. Until we let go, we will continue to hurt ourselves by our feelings concerning those who have wronged us.

Some people spend their lives seeking revenge. Some end up being victims, wallowing in how they have been mistreated by life's cruelties. Some people believe that they should never forgive, or it will happen again, and their lack of forgiveness infests their minds and hearts with bitterness. This bitterness shows on the face, especially around the mouth of an unforgiving person who is determined to hold on to her grudges for life.

We can all learn to forgive and do it without condoning the actions we are forgiving. Forgiveness is a way of reaching out from a bad past and heading out to a more positive future. Revenge may be sweet in prospect, but it sours the stomach. The longest journey by far is one that takes us from the head to the heart, and forgiveness is the short cut. Forgiveness is not a feeling. It is an act of will.

The stories we tell ourselves about the past keep us trapped. In our minds, we exaggerate what happened or change what happened to be more believable and to give ourselves permission to stay mad, to get revenge, or to stay stuck in our victim role. We may have experienced some tidal waves in our young lives, and in past relationships, but those few big waves are not the whole ocean. The ocean of life is vast, and if we will dive under the waves, or jump over them, and know that the person we're blaming for our suffering was acting out of her own pain, we can more easily forgive her.

We've been molded like wax by our parents, and our own awareness of their pain can soften the wax and enable us to mold our lives the way we choose. Under all the wax, once we've softened it and become pliable, is our very soul.

Sally, whose mother's natural voice still sounds

harsh to her on long distance phone calls, asked, "What if someone continues to offend or mistreat me?" Consider Jesus' response when Peter asked him how many times he should be willing to forgive his brother. "Seven times?" asked Peter. "Not seven times," replied Jesus, "but seventy times seven." Every spiritual teacher from Jesus to Mother Teresa has stated the simple answer: to love one another, offer pardon where there is hatred, and help where there is need.

Forgiveness is a spiritual practice. It is for our own sake even more than for others, and it leads directly to inner peace. This does not mean you stay in a verbally or physically abusive relationship with a lover, or employer, or a grown child. It means you forgive yourself for accepting the abuse in the past, you forgive the abuser for using you as an outlet for her rage instead of taking responsibility for herself. You do the therapy to heal the relationship, or you leave in peace. Some unforgiving people spend their lives blaming their parents, which keeps them stuck in the past, so they do not come fully into the present and rise to their full potential. As Nancy Friday says, "Blaming our parents is just a negative way of clinging to them still."

A Course in Miracles says, "When you have learned to look on everyone with no reference at all to the past, either his or yours as you perceive it, you will be able to learn from what you see now.[7] For the past is gone; the future but imagined. These concerns are but defenses against present change of focus in perception.[8] The present is the only time there is."[9]

"But," asks Sally, "am I supposed to forget that my mother said such cruel things to me when I was eleven or twelve years old?"

"What was going on in her life when you were eleven or twelve?" I asked.

"My father left her suddenly for a younger woman, and she fell apart," answered Sally.

"So her heart was broken, and she lost control of her words, and you must have been the closest one around for her to use as a sounding board for her own anger and hopelessness," I said.

"I just realized something," said Sally, surprised. "I liked his new girlfriend. She was like a girlfriend to play with, and she and my father let me do anything I wanted with them, and my mother knew that. I was so rebellious at home. It must have been hard for her. But I still can't forget the names she called me!"

"Sally", I said, with a new understanding. "Now that you know your mother was in so much pain, even if you're not ready to forget what happened, you can let go of the emotional charge that's connected with the memories. Maybe now you can remember some of the good things you received from your mother, and even appreciate the times she's reached out to you with love since you've grown up and she has healed. Was there good in your life when you were little before her time of unforgiveness of your father?"

"Yes," said Sally. "She nursed me as a baby, and all the time I was growing up she would kiss my neck and say, 'I want some honey from you, Sweet Honey.' She made a pink and red room for me with a toy closet and a clothes closet. She took me lots of places, and every day after school I had little girl friends over to play dress up."

"Sally," I said, "we all have selective memories. Without forgiveness, we only remember our hurts. When we accept forgiveness, we remember the good and that's our healing."

Today Sally and her mother are truly friends. They've shared life stories neither knew, and her happy mother and her stepfather have Sally, her husband and their children to spend joyful summers on their farm.

Dr. Jerry Jampolsky, founder of The Centers for Attitudinal Healing* and author of *Love is Letting Go of*

* There are now 150 Centers for Attitudinal Healing in over 30 countries!

Fear and ten other books, says in his latest book, *Forgiveness*:

"Forgiveness releases us from so much. It stops our inner battles with ourselves. It allows us to stop recycling anger and blame.

Forgiveness allows us to know who we truly are. With forgiveness in our hearts, we can at last experience our true essence as love.

Forgiveness is the great healer that allows us to feel joined and at one with each other and all that is life.

Forgiveness has the power to heal both our inner and outer lives. It can change how we see ourselves and others. It can change how we experience the world. It can bring an end, once and for all, to the inner conflicts that so many of us carry around with us every moment of every day. ...

As a physician for more than forty years, I can recall people with a variety of illnesses—from back problems, to ulcers, to high blood pressure, and even to cancer—who have had many of their symptoms abate as they learned to forgive. I have been heartened in recent years to see research emerging that shows a relationship between forgiveness and health. We now know that lack of forgiveness-that is, clinging to anger, fear, and pain-does have a measurable impact on our bodies. These create tensions which affect the physiological systems that we are dependent on for health. They affect the circulation of blood in our bodies. They affect the efficiency of our immune systems. They put stress on our hearts, on our brains, and on virtually every organ in our bodies. Lack of forgiveness is indeed a health factor."

Jerry also says, "The happiest marriages are built on a foundation of forgiveness." He tells wonderful stories in his talks around the world, and here are two of my favorites:

"In 1998, Diane and I went to West Africa to consult with the Center for Attitudinal Healing in Accra. While we were there, the executive director of the center, Mary Clottey, told us this story:

"Mary is a teacher at a school located about two hours from the capital. In her teaching she spent a great deal of time helping her young students find ways to communicate with each other without anger and fighting. She emphasized the process of forgiveness. In fact, her students knew her as 'the forgiveness teacher.'

"There was a ten year old boy in the school who was a real terror. He fought with every one and disrupted everything around him. Wherever he went, he seemed to break things, though he never accepted any responsibility for what he did.

"One day he was caught red-handed stealing money from his teacher's purse. The school principal jumped in and called for an assembly. According to the tradition of the school, the boy would be whipped with a cane up on the stage where everyone in the school could watch. They would make an example of him in this way, and then he would be expelled.

"The entire school assembled in the auditorium where the caning was to take place. But as the boy was led out to be caned, Mary stood up. Just as she was about to say, 'Forgive him,' all the children around her leapt to their feet.

"'Forgive him! Forgive him! Forgive him!' the children chanted, until the whole assembly hall was ringing with the message.

"The boy stared out into the audience and then broke down and began to sob. Suddenly the whole climate of the assembly hall changed.

"In the end, the boy was never caned. Nor was he expelled. Instead, he was forgiven and loved. From that day forward, he has not gotten into a single fight, broken anything, stolen, or been disruptive in any way.

"At first, many people in the school believed that the principal's action of calling the assembly to punish the boy was harsh and unfair. But he was forgiven, too, and in the process the seeds were planted for a new, more loving environment in the school."

The second story also comes from Africa:
"When a person acts unjustly or irresponsibly in the Babemba tribe of South Africa, he is placed alone in the center of the village but is in no way prevented from running off.

"Everyone in the village stops working and gathers in a circle around the person who has been accused. Then each person, regardless of age, begins to tell the person in the center about all the good things he or she has done during his or her life.

"Everything that can be remembered about this person is described in great detail. All the accused's positive attributes, good deeds, strengths, and kindnesses are verbalized for their benefit. Each person in the circle does this in great detail.

"All the stories about this person are told with the utmost sincerity and love. No one is allowed to exaggerate events that happened, and everyone knows that they cannot make stories up. Nobody is insincere or sarcastic as they speak.

"This ceremony continues until everyone in the village has had his or her say about how they value this person as a respected member of their community. This process can go on for several days. In the end, the tribe breaks the circle, and a joyous celebration occurs as the person is welcomed back into the tribe.

"Through the eyes of love, which this ceremony so beautifully describes, we find only reunion and forgiveness. Each person in the circle, as well as the person who is standing in the center, is reminded that forgiveness gives us the opportunity to let go of the past and the fearful future. The person in the center is no longer labeled as a bad person or excluded from the community.

FORGIVENESS

Instead, they are reminded of the love that is within them and are joined with those around them."

Letting go of the game of guilt sets us free

Reprinted with Permission

A Course in Miracles says, "It is as sure that those who hold grievances will suffer guilt, as it is certain that those who forgive will find peace."[10]

There is a wonderful true story about a Catholic priest who lived in the Philippines, a much-loved man of God, who carried a secret burden of a long past sin. He had committed this so-called sin many years before during his time in seminary. No one else knew of it. There was a woman in his parish who claimed to have had visions in which she regularly spoke with the Holy Spirit and He with her. The priest was, of course, skeptical of her claim, so he said, "The next time you have one of these conversations with the Holy Spirit, ask Him what sin your priest committed while he was in seminary." The woman agreed and went home.

When she returned to church a few days later, the

priest said, "Well, did the Holy Spirit visit you? And did you ask Him what sin I committed in seminary?" "Yes, I asked Him," she said. "He answered, 'I don't remember.'"

We can only make someone wrong in the past. As Jon Mundy says in *The Holy Encounter* (A Course in Miracles Magazine): "We do not understand forgiveness, for we believe that error must be met with punishment instead of love. Yet, all we learn through punishment is a deeper sense of guilt."

As A Course in Miracles says, "All healing is release from the past."[11]

Reprinted with Permission

FORGIVENESS

Here is a story I heard that exemplifies forgiveness:

A small boy at a summer camp received a box of cookies in the mail from his mother. He ate a few, then placed the remainder under his bed. The next day, after lunch, he went to his tent to get a cookie. The box was gone. That afternoon a camp counselor, who had been told of the theft, saw another boy sitting in the woods eating the stolen cookies. He said to himself, "That young man must be taught not to steal." He returned to the group and sought out the boy whose cookies had been stolen. He said. "I know who stole your cookies. Will you help me teach him a lesson?"

The puzzled boy replied "Well, yes, but aren't you going to punish him?"

The counselor explained, "No, that would only make him hate you and resent me. I want you to call your mother and ask her to send you another box of cookies."

He did as the counselor asked and a few days later received another box of cookies.

The counselor said, "Now, the boy who stole your cookies is sitting down there by the lake. Go down and share your cookies with him."

The boy protested, "But he's the thief."

"I know. But try it—see what happens."

Half an hour later the counselor saw the two boys coming up the hill, arm in arm. The boy who had stolen the cookies was earnestly trying to get the other to accept his pocket knife in payment for the stolen cookies, and the other was just as earnestly refusing the gift from his new friend, saying that a few cookies weren't all that important.

In an article titled *The Holy Spirit - Our Brothers, Our Sisters & Ourselves*, Jon Mundy tells this beautiful story: "I read a story which says something about the great need there is in this world for forgiveness. It seems there were a father and son in Madrid, Spain, whose relationship had become strained. The boy ran away from home. The father began a search for his rebellious son, to no avail. Finally, in a last desperate effort to find him, the father put a large ad in bold print in the newspaper and let it run for several days. The ad read:

Dear Paco, meet me in front of the newspaper office Saturday at noon. All is forgiven. I love you. Your father.

The next Saturday at noon, in front of the newspaper office, there were gathered together over one hundred young men named Paco."

Reprinted with Permission

Now we must talk about physical health for a minute. Our minds and bodies are connected. Forgiveness can keep us healthy. When you don't forgive, your anger festers into hate. Mentally and emotionally processing and obsessing about an unforgiven event drains energy. As you sincerely forgive, you let go of that negative energy and make room for love. Need I say more?

Now that you are ready for the journey into enlightenment, I invite you and your partner to make a forgiveness date for an evening or an afternoon. Plan to set aside three hours. Send the children to Grandma's or overnight to friends, or have a baby sitter. You and your partner go out in nature, to your office or a hotel room. Nothing can be more important than forgiving yourselves, each other and starting anew with a clean slate. Forgiveness is better for your health, your children, your business, your creative energies, and everyone you come in contact with.

And we begin! Light some sweet smelling candles, turn the lights low, turn on some meditative, peaceful music, turn off the phone and the idiot box. Sit close facing each other.

PART I
(Adapted from A Course in Miracles)

I would like you both to visualize all the hurtful memories from your past extending behind you on a long strip of carpet. Ask yourself the following questions:
- Do I truly want to be happy?
- Do I truly want to be peaceful?
- Do I truly want to experience love?
- Do I truly want to let go one hundred per cent of all my past grievances?

Then think of your partner or any person who you feel is responsible for blocking your awareness of peace and joy.

Now see yourself roll up the carpet and dispose of it. Allow yourself to experience the past as truly gone, and enjoy the opportunity for happiness in the present moment.

Now say: "This is my instant of releasing you (name), and myself from a guilty and unforgiving world. Together we can join in seeing a healed world free from guilt."

PART II

Now face each other with soft eyes, and take turns completing the following responses:
- My Script reasons (childhood wounds) for doing that were...
- The lesson I learned from doing that is...
- I'll never do that again, or
- I'll do therapy on that issue to make sure I never do that again.
- What can I do to help you to forgive me (and let go)?
What can I do so you'll feel safe that it won't happen again?

PART III

Now close your eyes and think of one quality, habit or personality trait that sometimes bothers you about your partner. Keeping your eyes closed, meditate on each question, and then take all the time you need to write your answers in the journal pages at the end of this chapter:
- What could be the lesson in that for you?
- Why did you attract this person to you on a soul level?
- If you were in perfect spiritual harmony right now, what would you do differently in this relationship?
- What new quality in you is wanting to emerge?

PART IV

Now from complete forgiveness through healing to love. Face your partner and complete these sentence stems:
- The hard lessons for me that I have learned from our

past difficulties are...Thank you for that gift...
- My childhood wounds that cause difficulties in our relationship that I take responsibility for are...
- One thing that I have criticized you about and tried to get you to change that I am going to let go of is... I take responsibility to be all right with you continuing to do (or not do) that.
- I have invented this situation as I see it.
- I am never upset for the reason I think.
- I completely forgive you for everything that has happened in the past and I will never bring it up again. The past is over, the future but imagined. These are but defenses against present change. Now is the only time there is."
- I am learning unconditional love.

Then hug and kiss each other. From this day forward you can decide to light each other's candle and to light each other's way through life, remembering to end each day forgiving each other for any transgressions, as the dear, wise, bearded, deep-voiced Rabbi Zalman Shalomi-Schachter taught us twenty years ago. A Course in Miracles says, "As forgiveness allows love to return to my awareness, I will see a world of peace and safety and joy."[12]

© Nicole Hollander, Reprinted with Permission

A Course in Miracles says, "Lay forgiveness on your mind and let all fear be gently laid aside, that love may find its rightful place in you.[13] To be born again is to let the past go, and look without condemnation upon the present.[14] You who want peace can find it only by complete forgiveness."[15]

"Turn your face to the sun and the shadow will fall behind you."—ancient Maori proverb

—Notes—

—Notes—

11

Vintage Love Growing Older —and Younger!— Together

"It takes a long time to become young."
—Pablo Picasso

    Together we blaze through the jungle, frolicking in refreshing waterfalls; then we eat lunch on a chaise lounge beach rock with a charming red cardinal as he chirps to the tune of the surf, thanking us for the crumbs of our Maui onion macadamia nut bread. Our afternoon delight is swimming as part of a pod of playful dolphins as only we dolphins do so spiritedly in our secret cove! Whatever we are doing, my domesticated husband, Cap'n Easy, and I rejoice in our soul connected love for each other and for life. Our relationship is vital and stimulating, and although we never run out of things to talk about, we also treasure our hours of silence sitting by the sea, as we watch the clouds with silver linings.
    Later at home we nourish each other with delicious fresh island fish poached in rosy champagne, with succulent garlic potatoes, and crispy fresh salad greens produced by the friendly Maui farmer/rebellious Council member down the road. We eat on our deck and watch the bright crimson sun set into the emerald ocean. For dessert, we're awed by the blazing pink, lavender and red

sky, while feeding each other and breathing in the aroma of fresh warm brown cinnamon apple pie with vanilla, raisins and crunchy macadamia nuts. After music, poetry, and listening to the Mark Twain of our time, Garrison Keilor, we nestle into each other on our porch swing, hold hands, and watch the full tangerine moon hanging in the night sky. Feeling so connected, we breathe the sensual fragrance of night-blooming jasmine beside the steps and trade greetings with the geckos who bring us luck.

My dear Angel Bub and I are playmates for laughing and romping together, nurturing parents to each other—"Honey, did you take your vitamins?"—adult companions, and work mates. Beyond the primitive need for symbiotic fusion, the most basic desire in a vintage relationship is for a soul connection. The transition from romantic hormonal love through the Power Struggle Stage to Conscious Vintage Love is an awakening to a love that grows deeper and more passionate with age. We were in such a hurry when we were young! Ah youth! Wisdom takes time. Love takes time. Our conscious, sacred, slowed-down, sensual, magical, total lovemaking gives us generous, total body orgasms and yet goes beyond bodily ecstasy to a soul connection that restores our youth, generates our health, opens our hearts, creates a profound bond, and manifests heaven on earth. Will Durant said, "The love that we have in our youth is superficial compared to the love that an old man has for his wife."

The way to have an interesting and exciting vintage marriage is to be interesting and exciting people, who surprise each other with new ideas and unexpected actions. Some of the secrets of wise person training are to stretch your curious mind by delving deeply into a variety of interests. Keep learning new things; be passionately involved in making the world a better place; stretch your sense of humor by noticing the humor in ordinary situations; and read, read, read. My husband's T-shirt says, "So Many Books, So Little Time." John Milton said, "A good book is the precious life-blood of a master-spirit, embalmed and treasured up on purpose to a life beyond life." Charles Kingsley said, "Except a living man, there is nothing more wonderful than a book! A message to us from...human souls we never saw...And yet these arouse us, terrify us, teach us, comfort us, open their hearts to us as brothers." And Samuel Johnson said, "Life long readers find in books the means to enjoy life or to endure it."

So I've digressed—my point is grow 'til you go! Now that I'm an elder in Wise Person Training I'm allowed to digress and—guess what!—people still listen with respect and attention! I like being an older woman—married to a wise, kind, handsome, funny and sexy—to digress a bit more—older man. What I'm getting to is: the golden years are rich when you have a loving companion with whom to share the wealth—and I don't mean money. When the Power Struggle stage was so long ago you can hardly remember what you argued about, you can put your creative energy into love, service and—well—writing a book! As Zora Neale Hurston, one of the first African-American women literary giants said, "there are years that ask questions and years that answer." Experience and learning from mistakes have given us a profusion of answers. So does communing with nature, away from the sounds of thoughtless chatter, heart-thumping traffic, and mind-numbing consumerism.

Graca Machal, age 51, the Minister of Education and the widow of the President of Mozambique, was quoted as saying about Nelson Mandela, "Oh, all right, I thought that part of my life was over, and here I am in love."

LATE AFTERNOON AT THE BEACH

I love the special stillness in the air
    on late afternoons at the beach.
The sun glistens the emerald ocean.
The palm trees sway
    to the gentle music of the surf.
The birds are singing in tune.

Husband, love of my life,
    thank you for sharing another
    sacred afternoon.
                —Natalie Tyler

    An 80 year old Taita man recalled his fourth wife with the words, "She was the wife of my heart."
    Indries Shaw said, "The most fundamental mistake people make is to think we are really alive when we have fallen asleep in life's waiting room," and the great Sufi poet, Kabir, wrote: "Jump into experience while you are alive...What you call 'salvation' belongs to the time before death...What is found now is found then. If you find nothing now, you will simply end up with an apartment in the City of Death. If you make love with the divine now, in the next life you will have the face of satisfied desire."
    "When you do talk, what on earth do you talk about after spending your whole day together and being married all these years?" asked Teresa, the concert violist in my WOW—Wild Outrageous Women—group. Well, Teresa, and all you other WOW's, here's the apple pie. I kept track for one typical week of what we talked about, and here in pie form are small, medium and large slices of our conversation topics.

VINTAGE LOVE
GROWING OLDER—& YOUNGER!—TOGETHER 207

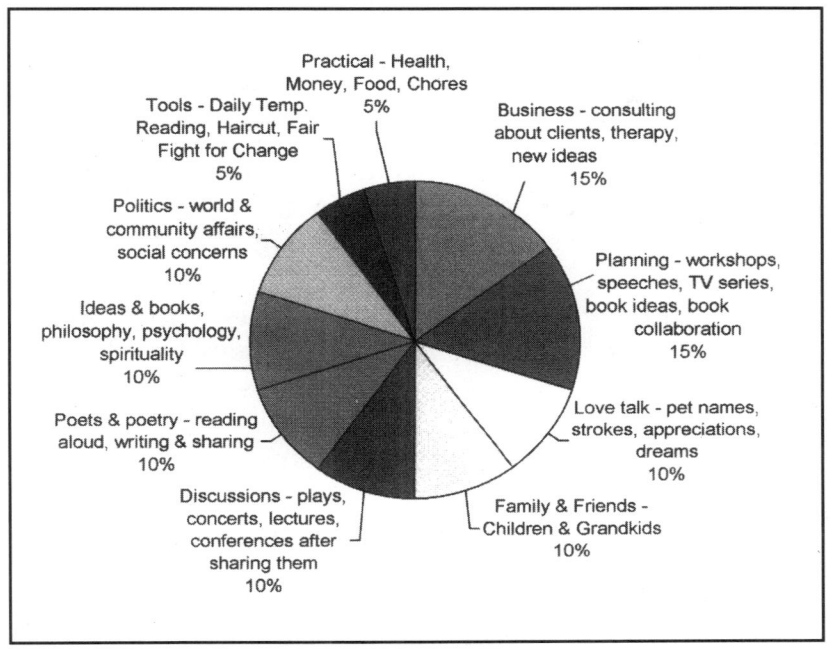

May I invite you to make a pie of your own conversation topics, and you might learn what to slice in larger or smaller pieces. Speaking of pies, be sure to stay 'til the last chapter for my other apple pie recipe with raisins, lemon and macadamia nuts—delicious!

So my message is—the more interests you have, the more interesting you are and the more aliveness you bring to your shared life!

• No one grows old by the number of years she lives.
• We grow old when we give up ideals and interests and zest for life.
• We grow old from a lack of touching and a lack of love.
• We get wrinkled souls when we lose our enthusiasm.
• We stay happy and feel young when we expand our thinking and deepen our feelings.
• We stay young when we accept our wrinkled skin and unwrinkle our hearts.

Carolyn Heilbrun writes, in *The Last Gift of Time—Life Beyond Sixty*: "Now that I feel my life to be brief in time, do I seek to extend it in weight. I try to delay the velocity of its flight by the velocity with which I grasp it, and to compensate for the speed of its collapse by the zest which I throw into it. The shorter my hold on life, the deeper and fuller do I seek to render it. Others feel the sweetness of contentment and well being. I feel it just as much as they do, but not by letting it just slip away."

We've all heard these up and coming words:

"First I was dying to finish high school and start college.

And then I was dying to finish college and start working.

And then I was dying to marry and have children.

And then I was dying for my children to grow old enough for school so I could return to work.

And then I was dying to retire.

And now, I am dying...and suddenly I realize I forgot to live."

—Anonymous

I invite you to underline those words, copy them, magnet them to your refrigerator door, frame them, *even* cut them out of this book, and then go do something you've been "dying" to do all your life—even come to Maui! If you're already here in Paradise, go to Amsterdam or Venice; invite someone from a different culture to tea; feed the homeless; go up in a balloon; take classes you've always wanted to take; become politically involved.

WORK

Work is important. Work contributes to our personal identity by helping define who we are. It also provides a sense of community through its network of supportive relationships. And meaningful work enriches our lives by giving us a sense of purpose—we feel that our lives matter. It is important to do work we feel called to do. Thomas Moore says, in the July, 1997 edition of *Moving Books*: "To pay attention to that call is paying attention to the inner voice, or reading the world around you to determine where you should go, instead of taking an aptitude test or going where the most money is. If everyone followed their calling, I think we'd undergo quite a transformation in our world. The other thing is to do work that really satisfies your heart, that somehow fulfills your sense of destiny."

Retiring from needing to work for money is a golden opportunity to volunteer your services in total commitment for a life-enhancing meaningful purpose. Thomas Henry Huxley said, "the great end of life is not knowledge but action."

Knowledge is illuminating, and the next step is action! Years ago I thought aging was about limits. Now I know it's about stretching beyond our limits to freedom. I hear what you're thinking: "You haven't mentioned health or sex yet, and that's what I want to hear about in a chapter with the phrase 'growing old' in it." Well, I'm glad you asked, and they do go together!

There's an ancient proverb that says, "An old man in love is like a flower in winter." Good, regular sex, which includes enormous amounts of long, drawn out tender touching, keeps us healthy. According to Dr. Bernie Siegel, "Love boosts the immune system more than any vitamin, medication or alternative treatment." I feel and am years younger than what my birth certificate says.

MY SECRETS

• Sacred sex. See Chapter 8.
• Bonding every day and night. See Chapter 8.
• Weekly massages.
• Laughing uncontrollably every day—that inner jogging is powerful!

- Reading, learning and discovering new ideas, people, places, activities regularly.
- High Energy Fun. See Chapter 9.
- Romantic surprises.
- Poetry.
- Meditating in nature.
- Joyful fulfilling work. "We are shaped and fashioned by what we love."—Johann Wolfgang von Goethe.
- Creating an environment using Feng Shui magic, artful colors, fragrant scents, harmonic sounds, wondrous visions of nature, and many bodily delights—soft flannel sheets, sweet smelling bouquet of bubble baths, mango body lotion, riding the ocean waves, and touching that familiar, comforting body of my beloved. The philosopher, Epicurus, stated that "pleasure is the most important virtue."
- Service to our community and to the larger community—the wonderful world we inhabit. Ghandi said, "It doesn't matter how small a thing you do, it matters that you do it."
- Exercising our bodies daily—not inside on a machine, but out in fresh, unpolluted air. Walt Whitman wrote, "If anything is sacred, the human body is sacred." Isak Dinesen said, "The cure for anything is salt water—sweat, tears or the sea."
- Close friendships between those of sufficiently different generations offer unusual wisdom and generous understanding of life. Spending valuable, precious time with young people—the younger they are the closer we come to meeting God. Spending precious, meaningful time with old people, and ask questions of the wise ones. The older they are, the closer we come to meeting God. Without cross generation close relationships, we live in a state of righteous ignorant self-satisfaction, lacking awareness of so much.
- Eating generous amounts of *fresh* vegetables, fruits, and cell-regenerating, life-extending fresh fish. We don't

VINTAGE LOVE
GROWING OLDER—& YOUNGER!—TOGETHER 211

drink coffee, eat red meat, or white flour, but we eat lots of chocolate, because we don't deprive ourselves of anything we really love in these Golden Years! Also a cold bottle of champagne goes so well with the sunset.

• Collecting and maintaining (friendship requires maintenance) a few good, trustworthy, wise friends. A friend is someone who knows your vices, frailties and bad habits, and still accepts you as you are, believes in you, and loves you. A friend is someone with whom you feel safe to say anything without being judged or rejected. Emerson said, "A friend is someone before whom I may think aloud."

• Voyaging on a spiritual path that connects you to Spirit, or your Higher Self. The most exciting and longest journey is the journey within to discover yourself. This does not necessarily mean organized religion or a church or synagogue or temple, although it is part of spirituality for some. More than anything, it means letting go of judgments and seeing God in every being, in every tree, in all God's creatures—on land, in air or sea. It means replacing needing to be right with choosing to be kind. It means eliminating greed and replacing working for more money than needed with "How can I serve?" It means seeing God in all her disguises. Wayne Dyer says, "The only measure of what your life was about will be 'How did I give it away?'"

• Expressing gratitude each day. William Arthur Wood said, "Feeling gratitude and not expressing it is like wrapping a present and not giving it."

Reprinted with Permission of King Features Syndicate, Hagar the Horrible

We can choose how we want to be in the world. We're fortunate to be living in a society where we have a wide range of choices. How we respond to the circumstances we find ourselves in is up to us.

A Course in Miracles says, "*Now* is the closest approximation of eternity that this world offers. It is in the reality of 'now', without past or future, that the beginning of the appreciation of eternity lies."[1]

Here are two of my favorite Christmas newsletters sent by Rose and Bruce Bliven in 1975 at age 86 and 1976 at 87. He was the editor of The New Republic for 30 years. Here's the first one:

"At 86, Rose and I live by the rules of the elderly. If the toothbrush is wet, you have brushed your teeth. If the bedside radio is warm in the morning, you left it on all night. If you are wearing one brown shoe and one black shoe, you have another pair just like it somewhere in the closet.

"I stagger when I walk, and small boys follow me, making bets on which way I'll go next. This upsets me. Small boys shouldn't gamble. Like most elderly people, we spend many happy hours in front of the TV set. We rarely turn it on."

Here's a condensed version of their Christmas letter the following year:

"Dear friends: Rosie and I are now 87. Would we care to try for 174? The answer is no. I'm 46 percent as old as the United States and still can't spell 'seize'.

"Rosie has aged some in the past year and now seems like a woman entering her 40s. Last May we celebrated our 63rd wedding anniversary. When we are old, the young are kinder to us and we are kinder to each other. There is a sunset glow that radiates from our faces and is reflected on the faces of those about us. But still, it is sunset."

All the research teaches us that married couples

VINTAGE LOVE
GROWING OLDER—& YOUNGER!—TOGETHER

enjoy more emotional and physical security than singles or uncommitted couples, and that being married leads to a greater life expectancy, less illness, less stress, and better household income. In short, Pat Truly, columnist and editorial writer for the Fort Worth Star Telegram, says, "Being married beats the heck out of not being married."

Your living is determined not so much by what life brings to you as by the attitude you bring to life, not so much by what happens to you as by the way your mind looks at what happens. Circumstances and situations do color life, but you have been given the mind to choose what the color shall be. Becoming conscious in relationship is like finally stumbling out of a dark narrow tunnel and floating, skipping, flying, sailing, and dancing to freedom and enlightenment!

There's an old Greek proverb that says, "The heart that loves is forever young." Life together is easier as we grow older and become mellower, and finally acquire a mature perspective on what is important and what is "Oops, no big deal." We give our clients the assignment to say "Oops, no big deal"* at least 5 times a day! As we look back on all the things we worried about in our younger years that now seem irrelevant, we let go of needing to be perfect, and of the idea that money is the path to happiness. As our wise person training progresses, we learn that happiness has to do with loving and being loved and cherished, self esteem, a sense of being in control of our lives, optimism, forgiveness, friendship, spirituality and service. If you can learn to love a flawed creature, you can learn to love yourself. Whatever the question, unconditional love is the answer.

The other night, sitting on our porch swing listening to *Prairie Home Companion*, we heard Garrison Keilor say, "As you grow older, you spend more time thinking about the hereafter—when you go downstairs to look for something,

---

* We learned "Oops, no big deal from HeartMath®, by Doc Lew Childre

you think 'What am I here after?'" It's beginning to happen in our house—I won't say who the sweet person is with the affliction—and it's cozy to laugh together at our charming signs of getting a little older. I suppose in 10 years we'll be even more forgetful, but wiser. Wisdom is an even better gift than a good memory. When we Golden Agers have collected so much information and acquired so much knowledge over so many years and so many experiences, it's natural that there's not quite enough room in our crowded brains to remember where we put the car keys, who just called, or what time the dinner party starts.

• In general, happiness in the Golden Years seems to encompass five main areas:
• An ability to adapt to changing circumstances.
• A view of the world as benevolent and controllable.
• Values, work and goals that provide a sense of direction.
• Love, friendship, service and community.
• Spiritual fulfillment, whether that means spending time in nature, in church or temple, reading and writing poetry, or simply practicing loving kindness.

PEANUTS reprinted by permission of United Feature Syndicate

Jean Cocteau wrote, "Picasso told me that he had seen in Avignon, on the square of the Chateau des Papes, an old painter, half-blind, who was painting the castle. His wife, standing beside him, looked at the castle through binoculars and described it to him. He was painting from his wife."

MARRIED LOVE

You and I
Have so much love
That it
Burns like a fire,
In which we bake a lump of clay
Molded into a figure of you
And a figure of me.
Then we take both of them,
And break them into pieces,
And mix the pieces with water,
And mold again a figure of you
And a figure of me.
I am in your clay.
You are in my clay.
In life we share a single quilt.
In death we will share one bed.
—Kuan Tao-Sheng

Translated by Kenneth Rexroth
and Ling Chung

"It isn't death that's the enemy, but the closed heart. Love is the optimum strategy for healing."
—Stephen Levine

"Heaven is here.
There is nowhere else.
Heaven is now.
There is no other time."[2]
　　　　—A Course in Miracles

VINTAGE LOVE
GROWING OLDER—& YOUNGER!—TOGETHER

—Notes—

—Notes—

PART III

EVERYTHING ELSE

YOU NEED TO KNOW

12

Healthy, Happy People
Healthy, Happy Couples
Healthy, Happy Families

"The last of the human freedoms--to choose one's attitude in any given set of circumstances, to choose one's own way."
—Viktor Frankl

During our courting days, Cap'n Easy and I once sent each other the same greeting store card—they crossed in the mail—that's when we decided we were star-crossed lovers. The picture on the front of our identical cards depicted two beautiful aging people sitting in rocking chairs on a homey front porch looking out at their garden. The inside said, "Come grow old with me. The best is yet to be.—Robert Browning."

As we sit on our porch swing gazing at the pastel palette of the sky—the scenic background behind our hanging porch plants of red impatiens, purple petunias and yellow nasturtiums, and above our purple orchid tree and giant green mango tree—I realize that I have written this second act of my life. My parents wrote the first half of the play by the scenes they set. I dreamed, fantasized, visualized, plotted and planned the second half. I think it was Einstein who said you have to be able to imagine something first before you can materialize it. Wayne Dyer wrote *You'll See It When You Believe It*. As we sit on our porch swing, I think back to that card we sent each other, and together we reminisce about our beginnings those many years ago.

I sent Blue Rivers that card after our third date, because I'd always dreamed of having a front porch for just plain sitting with my romantic cozy old fashioned husband—a man I made up in my fantasies during my dating days, and during my marriage to the shallow, dull man, who didn't know what a feeling was, the one everyone who wasn't married to him thought was so nice. Now here we are, the deep man and I, happily cuddling on our porch, swinging and watching the trees.

In the card, the two sweet old people were sitting in rocking chairs on the porch. I'm glad we have a swing instead, because his shoulder is such a good pillow! I call it my "pillow willow." We are reminiscing about the Circle Supper at our house last night, and how profound the conversation was from beginning to end. Everyone followed our instructions and brought a story or poem or experience to share in the circle on our enormous play pen couch after dinner. Bonnie, Chick and Nancy read poetry, Gayook read from her published book of poems, *Bridge Across My Soul*, Jeanne read an unforgettable story, Valerie explained to us the profound connection between her professional practice as a physician and her spiritual healing gifts. Norm shared an exciting travel adventure, LeClaire enthralled us with stories of her teaching career, John read one of his Whale poems, and I read a few pages from my Sexuality chapter—by popular demand.

What a stimulating evening of mind and heart connections! If I had stayed in Cincinnati for the rest of my life, I would have mostly known people just like me. I cannot imagine how limited that would have been for me—staying forever where I was planted. How enriching it is to know—really know well—people from such different cultures. None of us is here by accident—we all chose to move here to Maui because of a sense of place.

Jeanne hails from France and Holland, Gayook from China, Valerie from Montana, Nancy and Bonnie from California, Chick and LeClaire African Americans from Detroit, Norm from Australia, and we, the hosts, from Connecticut and Cincinnati via Massachusetts.

We all have had such different experiences, and yet we seem so alike in our search for meaning—even though our ages range from 40 to 75—or who knows? Well, here we are porch sitters re-enjoying last night, and I am again re-enjoying it with you. It's time for the moral to this story: *friends are important*. Laughing friends are fun, intellectual friends are stimulating, adventure friends are companionable—and sometimes you can get all of these and a soul connection to boot!

Shared friendship is a gratifying way to grow—not old or young—but deeper together on a shared life journey.

A healthy person is someone who enjoys a quality, balanced life, can separate the trivial from the important, can laugh at himself, has surrendered the need to control, judge or manipulate others, and takes responsibility for his own thoughts, feelings and actions.

A balanced life includes right livelihood, service to others, play and recreation, friendships, learning (which includes reading, learning new things and sharing ideas), health care (physical exercise, nutrition, body care, professional medical, naturopathic or chiropractic when necessary and psychotherapy for healing childhood wounds and current emotional stress), spirituality, contact with nature and intimate love. A balanced life is free from addictions.

Emotionally healthy people take responsibility for their own actions instead of blaming others. A Course in Miracles says: "I am responsible for what I see. I choose the feelings I experience, and I decide upon the goal I would achieve. And everything that seems to happen to me I ask for, and receive as I have asked."[1]

If we are willing to learn from our negative experiences, we can use them for healthy growth and happiness. The Chinese ideograph for "crisis" is "danger + opportunity". We can learn to use crisis as a challenge. We can say in difficult times, "What is the lesson in this for me." Our colleague, Dr. Elaine Childs-Gowell, calls such a difficult time an AFGO—Another Fucking Growth Opportunity. If we are open to whatever may happen, we won't have tunnel vision. Mary Pipher says, "Stress is what a person decides is stressful."

Pir Vilayat Inayat Khan, who brought Sufism to our western world, says, "Your pain is the breaking open of the shell that enclosed your understanding." Taking responsibility for what we make happen takes courage, which is grace under pressure. G.K. Chesterton said, "Courage is the power of being cheerful in circumstances we know to be desperate." Another definition of courage is being afraid and doing it anyhow.

Part of the healthy happy life is finally growing up and learning how to manage pain. Ethel Barrymore said, "You grow up the day you have the first real laugh at yourself." Laughter is inner jogging. Dr. Jerry Jampolsky says, "Laughter is an inner hug." I guess how hard you laugh depends on whether it is a healthy hug or healthy jogging.

Healthy, happy people live in the present and have an abundance of energy and awareness for *Here* and *Now*. When some of our energy is stuck in anger and guilt about the past and some caught up in fear about the future, there is not enough left over to be fully in the present.

HEALTHY, HAPPY PEOPLE... HEALTHY, HAPPY COUPLES... HEALTHY, HAPPY FAMILIES

DUNAGIN'S PEOPLE

"I CAN'T STOP THINKING ABOUT TOMORROW."

At the end of our therapy workshop, Angel Bub and I fly up our steps surrounded by walls and ceiling covered with pictures of all of our kids and grandkids. We settle together on our huge yellow snuggle couch that our dear friend, Lois, calls the playpen. We gaze at the purple and green comforting spectacle outside of our screened windowless walls. The purple bougainvillea is asking to come closer to us, climbing and winding through the fairyland fluff of cascading green leaves of our kiawe tree, caressing our screens. After sharing some Maui pineapple wine, my best friend, co-therapist, silly playmate husband retreats to the koa wood kitchen to make his pesto pasta specialty with fresh basil, pine nuts, olive oil, cilantro, garlic and black olives. As Kim in my WOW (Wild Outrageous Women!) group says, "It's fun to be the queen!" I join him to make fresh salad out of everything in the refrigerator drawer.

We take our plates out to the deck to our round table with the Hawaiian tablecloth, and we listen to the folksy voice of Garrison Keilor on our moveable speakers. We enjoy the vision on this side of our book lined cozy treetop living room. It is a little wilder, but same color scheme. Our purple orchid tree has spread throughout our vision, towering over our yellow plumeria, fuchsia plumeria, papaya, orange and lemon trees. We express gratitude to each other for being smart enough and courageous enough to risk the unknown and fly across the ocean to Paradise.

Prairie Home companion ends and we return to the snuggle couch. John picks up the front page of yesterday's cozy island newspaper, and I start with Doonesbury in the comics. We work our way to the middle and trade sections. I read, "Variety of friends might be a way to keep colds away, study indicates." It is true! Friends are important.

When I finish this book, I am going to spend more time with friends and write the next book more slowly. In fact, health and slow are bunk mates. When we slow down, we pay attention to our own needs and desires, we hear the children, and we smell the familiar fragrance of our lover's skin and taste the delicious sweet love oozing from every pore.

Healthy, happy people have the capacity for love, and for compassion and empathy. Before we can love others, we need to love ourselves. There must be enough self-love to sustain love. Many people unconsciously think, "I couldn't love anyone dumb enough or desperate enough to love me."

Our first task is to love ourselves and—yes—we *can* learn to do that! Even those of us who were not loved enough in childhood can at last learn to love and cherish ourselves.

GUIDELINES ON HOW TO LOVE YOURSELF

- Forgive yourself for all past mistakes. You did the best you could do with the information and resources you had at the time. If you could have done any better you would have.
- Praise yourself. Criticism breaks down the inner spirit; praise builds it up. Praise yourself as much as you can.

Tell yourself how well you are doing with every little thing.
- Do things you do well that you are proud of doing and complete the tasks.
- Find at least one friend, teacher, therapist or mentor who believes in your strengths, your goodness and your ability to manage your life.
- Find joyful livelihood, something you are good at, that you feel passionate about, that you look forward to each day. This is not about getting rich, but about daily satisfaction.
- Find a cause you believe in and give your support. Reach out each day to do something for someone else. Make regular anonymous gifts.
- Take care of your mind. Read. Read. Read. Read. Keep reading, growing, and learning new things the rest of your life.
- Find ways to support yourself. Reach out to friends and allow them to help you. You are being strong to ask for help when you need it.
- Lovingly release old negative patterns, acknowledge that you created them to fulfill a need, and then find new, positive ways to fulfill that need.
- Take care of your body. Learn about nutrition. What kind of fuel does your body need to have optimum energy and vitality? Learn about exercise. What kind of exercise can you enjoy? Cherish and revere the temple you live in.
- End all criticism and self-punishment. Criticism never changes a thing. Refuse to criticize yourself, and accept yourself exactly as you are. Everybody changes. When you criticize yourself, your changes are negative. When you approve of yourself, your changes are positive.
- Live a life of forgiveness.
- Nourish your soul with music, poetry, nature, little children, old people, and animals. Thomas Moore says, "We have to live from a very deep place to know the soul that is creating and unfolding our own individuality."

- Feel a sense of responsibility and belonging to the universe and in awe of being here. Albert Schweitzer says, "You know of the disease in Central Africa called sleeping sickness...there also exists a sleeping sickness of the soul. Its most dangerous aspect is that one is unaware of its coming. That is why you have to be careful. As soon as you notice the slightest sign of indifference, the moment you become aware of the loss of a certain seriousness, of longing, of enthusiasm and zest, take it as a warning. You should realize your soul suffers if you live superficially."

The best explanation I know of why some relationships are therapeutic and some are not comes from a Vietnamese proverb:

"While it is noble to assist a stricken elephant in rising, it is foolhardy to catch one that is falling down."

Two can live more deeply than one, and when two healthy, whole, deep people come together in love, they can be each other's soul guides. Relationships bring spirituality down to earth and into the home. How we treat each other is at the heart of our spirituality.

In a spiritual relationship we willingly do things for each other—we see this as giving instead of as deprivation. The more we reach out to each other for the purpose of mutual healing, the more human we become. Albert Einstein said, "The purpose of life is to become more fully human." When we acknowledge and respect our humanness, we start taking responsibility for ourselves, and stop blaming each other.

Instead of accusing your spouse and playing the blame game, a better alternative is to say, "I need help." The other person's heart usually opens if you ask for help, instead of attacking. "I need help" could mean, "I'm feeling crazy right now. I want you to stay sane and hear me out." It never works for both people to go crazy at the same time. If you can both remember that, the situation will not escalate and you each can stretch your empathy (good for the soul) and allow the other to be a little insane once in a while. If a baby cries and you go to pick him up, he usually stops crying, but if you ignore him or yell at him, he will cry longer and louder, and it will be harder to calm him down. Anger and attack are an adult's way of crying, so stop and listen and comfort immediately, and your partner's out of control hysteria, worry or criticism might melt down to become calm appreciation for your comforting ways.

Happiness is at the root of happy marriages and happy families. Happy people tend to look at the bright side, to see the glass half full, instead of half empty, even if that sometimes borders on being unrealistic. The positive does not need to be an illusion. People who make good things happen know that even bad news can be positive, if we can learn the lessons, change our path or strengthen our effort.

According to David Myers in *The Pursuit of Happiness: Who is Happy and Why*, "Happy people tend to be comfortable and pleased with themselves, interested in their work, likely to have many friends, a spouse, and a spiritual orientation. Happy people are generous people—in other words, people who spend as much time focusing on the happiness of others as they do worrying about the sufficiency of their own satisfaction."

Laughter is the language of happiness. It drains away tension, relaxes the veins, arteries, and respiratory system. It contracts the face muscles and stimulates the immune system. It is hard to argue, complain, or criticize while you are laughing!

So now let us get right down to it. If you have not had good role models, this is what happy couples look like:
• They have common interests as well as separate, individual interests. They have both shared and separate friends.
• They are flexible, not rigid. They coordinate mutual needs for dependence and independence based on self-

awareness, self-acceptance and self-esteem of both people. They are interdependent, rather than codependent, do not depend solely on the relationship to get their needs met, and take responsibility for their own happiness.
- They share power and have complementary roles. They encourage each other's growth, change, exploration and expression of autonomy.
- They bring out the best in each other and take responsibility for their own thoughts, feelings and behavior. They don't blame each other or try to change each other.
- They are available to be best friend, playmate, lover, parent, child and main emotional support system to each other, in various roles at different times.
- They have common values about the things most important to them—such as children, where to live, spirituality, politics, money.
- They create time to be alone together, and are both comfortable with intimacy. They play and laugh together often, prefer each other's company to any one else most of the time, and engage in a richly varied assortment of activities together.
- They are committed to each other's well being, and to healing each other's wounded child. They tell each other "I love you" often, and nurture each other regularly. They do daily Caring Behaviors, and demonstrate verbal and physical affection openly and frequently every day. They take care of each other during sickness and sadness.
- They communicate regularly, openly and honestly, sharing feelings, thoughts, ideas, plans and dreams, and listening carefully to each other.
- They are monogamous and sexually adventurous with each other.
- They accept each other's differences and limitations, are mostly free of power struggles, control issues, competition and score keeping. They recognize that conflict is inevitable in any intimate relationship, and they choose to "Fight Fair", without hostility or verbal or physical

abuse. Both remain open during conflict, staying on the Intent to Learn path (See Chapter 4), instead of the closed path of self-protection. They do not withdraw from each other without explaining
• They have a clear contract to stay together and resolve differences, seeking therapy when necessary, and don't threaten to leave. Both are equally committed to making the relationship work,
• They have no secrets. They trust each other completely and have transcended jealousy.
• They effectively solve problems together.
• Both are free of addictions.
• They respect and admire each other and each other's work, hobbies and interests.
• They have said "good-bye" to past lovers emotionally.
• They ask straight for 100% of what they want, and *do not rescue each other*.
• They make amends for unloving behaviors, and readily say, "I'm sorry".
• They love themselves even more when they're together.
• They share household tasks, and parenting if there are shared children.
• They make full financial disclosure to each other and make financial decisions equally.

Happy couples in healthy marriages generate happy families. Happy families spend time with each other and listen to each other. They are usually busy people with many divergent interests, but *they are not always busy*. The great Chinese philosopher, Lin Yutang, wrote, "If you can spend a perfectly useless afternoon in a perfectly useless manner, you have learned how to live."

What would it be like to spend fifteen hours in the home of a happy, healthy family? What would you notice? We visited our colleague, Marty Frank, and his boisterous family in Santa Cruz after an International Transactional Analysis Association Conference in San Francisco and a visit with our children in Berkeley. A bike and a dog guard the front door. We bump into Josh, age fourteen, dashing out. He stops in the middle of his dash to say, "Hi", politely shakes our hands, and tells us he will see us at dinnertime. We enter an open, exciting yet peaceful family circus.

Marty comes to the door with bear hugs, and Jane yells from the kitchen, "Welcome, come on in and taste this." April, age sixteen, and her friend, Ivy, are setting the table, both with earphones! We hear a thud upstairs, and Adam, nine, comes flying down the stairs screaming, "Zachary won't let me play." Marty says, "Then play with someone else or by yourself, if that's the way it is. I'm sorry." And he gives him a hug.

I talk to Jane and taste her shrimp scampi specialty, while John goes out to study their bookcase, a cool drink in his hand. Marty asks April and Ivy to gather up their books from the couch, and Adam to move his puzzle, then goes upstairs to give Zachary, age eleven, his ten minute notice to end his computer adventure and come help with dinner. Jane, April and Ivy sit down in the living room with us and tell us Frank family news. Marty gathers the boys in the kitchen to help dish out dinner.

Jane lights the candles, and we all hold hands as Marty says, "Bless this food, this house and everybody in it." At that moment Josh dashes in with, "I'm sorry I'm late! I accept the consequences. I'll clean up with whose ever turn it is." He sits down, piles enough food for an army on his plate and nothing more is said about it. Marty praises Jane for the delicious food, Jane marvels over Marty's homemade bread, and all the kids chime in, everybody talking at once as the food is passed with yummy noises all around. Then Jane rings a delicate gong (fork against glass), and everyone has a turn to tell the worst and best thing that happened to him that day. The phone rings about five times during dinner for this popular family. April explains to us that dinnertime is their sacred family time, and the family rule is to let the answering machine take calls.

After dinner everyone clears the table, Adam and Josh clean the kitchen, April goes to check the answering machine and make calls, while Ivy goes with Zachary to play a computer game. We four adults relax and talk. April interrupts to ask if she can go to a movie with Jacob. Jane and Marty look at each other for agreement, and Marty says, "Yes if you will be in the house by 11:00 p.m." Jane says, "Wait, you have Ivy for a guest. Are you being polite?" April says, "Yes, Ivy and Michael are coming with us." Jane says, "Have a good time," while Marty says, "What movie and who is driving?" That took five minutes to settle.

There is a feeling of openness, honesty and acceptance in this family that makes room for self esteem, safety, approval and love. The boys go up to get their supplies for sleeping out in their tent, so we can sleep in their room.

Once during our adult evening of laughs playing *Life Stories*, Adam comes in crying, scared by "a ghost out there." After hugs, reassurances and a bathroom reminder, he goes back out to join his brother. April and Ivy come home on the dot of 11:00 p.m. and tell us so much about the movie that we don't need to see it! John and I are sleepy. Marty gives Jane a kiss and says, "Let's go to bed, Honey." April says, "Good night, love birds" to her parents and to us. Kisses and hugs all around and a peaceful night's sleep.

In the morning after Marty's fresh orange juice and hearty pancakes, everyone is off in different directions with good-bye kisses and "See you at dinner." We give our heartfelt thanks and hugs. As we leave, Marty goes to clean up from breakfast, after which he and Jane have plans to hike together, then a family afternoon picnic.

There is so much we fondly remember about the Frank's house. There was a calm disarray, lots of laughter, hugs and kisses, compliments, and books. There were clear limits and respect. Family dinner time was family bonding time and everyone was heard. "I'm sorry" was a familiar expression. Everyone was flexible and no one stayed stuck in a position. Jane and Marty laughed at themselves often—Jane laughed at herself for worrying about April staying out until 11:00 p.m., and Marty goodnaturedly said, "The person who knows how to laugh at herself will never cease to be amused." We felt warm and comfortable and happy being in that home with that family.

On the way home Angel Bub remembered a poem by Jelaluddin Rumi, inspired by our friendship with the Franks: "Stay in the company of lovers. Those other kinds of people, they each want to show you something. A crow will lead you to an empty barn; a parrot to sugar."

And I remembered that H. Matthews said, "A man is too apt to forget that in this world he cannot have everything. A choice is all that is left him." A good idea is to have friends who are in happy, healthy families—it rubs off!

There is a spiritual dimension in the lives of healthy people, healthy couples, and healthy families. Spirituality is how we live—how we treat each other and our environment. We need to make our home a Sacred Place in our own unique way, with candles, peaceful music, plants, pets, an altar, fresh homemade bread, space for quiet meditation and hospitality to friends, and above all, laughter and joy. When parents seek and find meaning in their lives, they model this value for their children, not by sermons or lectures, but by placing soul at the center of life and by living as if all life and all people are precious expressions of God. This means cleaning up litter in the woods, parks, beaches and streams instead of adding to it, and having concern for others, including treating all animals with respect—have you noticed that DOG is GOD spelled backwards? As A Course in Miracles says, "When you meet anyone, remember it is a holy encounter."[2]

Children notice your attitude: when you are served

by a waiter who makes a human mistake; how polite you are to the noisy neighbors; and the look on your face when you pass a gay couple holding hands, or an African-American teenager with dreadlocks. Children are also strongly affected by whether you treat them as inferior know-nothings or as holy children of God. Parents who practice the spiritual life and have family rituals, including the important dinner hour with everyone attending and paying attention, provide important role modeling for their children.

Mary Pipher says, "Good families understand themselves and have strong value systems." Family life can be a vast palace of generosity, fun and humor, kindness, encouragement, gentleness, safety, cooperation, gratitude and courage. Sometimes we shut off all those rooms because we do not know they exist—we did not learn about them in our own childhood. Then we live in a three room apartment of fear, rigidity, and judgment. We are not used to the potential we have in family life, so the rooms of the castle become dusty from lack of use. We retreat into the shell we are used to because we think it is safe.

Second to love, flexibility may be the most important ingredient in family life. When we acknowledge how rigid we have become, we become more flexible. When we see how unconscious we have been, we become more conscious. The deeper we love, the more frightened we become of the very love we crave. Courage, Brave Hearts! Giving up our survival mechanisms seems like death, but death of mechanisms we no longer need is life, and love is what life is all about. Albert Einstein said, "There are two ways to live your life: one is as through nothing is a miracle; the other is as if everything is."

The bridge to health and happiness is to massage the wall around your heart by healing your childhood wounds, using the Parent/Child Dialogue in Chapter 3; asking for and giving Caring Behaviors as described in Chapter 7; forgiving yourself and all others, using the tools in

Chapter 10; and making time for fun. Begin now by acting as if you are an open-hearted, flexible, generous person, and your feelings will catch up to your actions.

Reprinted with Permission

Make a heart connection with your spouse and children by loving them exactly as they are. You are on the path to enlightenment. Your open heart has prepared you to make a soul connection now by loving your spouse and children for who they are and who they are becoming, and by knowing you have an important role in their development and they in yours.

Happy, healthy people have and continually seek meaning in their lives beyond the superficiality of buying things, controlling other people, watching the idiot box, and having rigid rules, or complete lack of rules. Enlightenment is the reward given to those who seek meaning. These people have a two-fold existence. They conscientiously perform their work in the world. And they are inwardly immersed in spiritual peace.

"The purpose of life is to be happy."
—The Dalai Lama

HEALTHY, HAPPY PEOPLE... HEALTHY, HAPPY COUPLES... HEALTHY, HAPPY FAMILIES 237

–Notes–

13

Conscious Parenting

"You must be the change you wish to see in the world."
—Mahatama Gandhi

CALVIN AND HOBBES © 1993. Watterson. Reprinted with permission of Universal Press Syndicate. All rights reserved.

It is a great privilege, an honor and a spiritual challenge to have children. One of the best ways to prepare for parenthood is to have had good parental role modeling in your childhood, and to have healed your own childhood wounds in therapy, so you do not pass the hot potato to your children. Another is to read good books and attend classes and workshops on parenting. One of the reasons for healing your childhood wounds is so your parenting energy is not bound up in unfinished business. You can be the parent you would have liked to have had.

A wise friend of mine said, "One of the greatest gifts my parents gave me was their love for each other." Children are more intuitive than most adults. They do not yet have the wide vocabularies, the sensory environmental overload, or the book learning we have, so their intuition is stronger. When there is tension in the parents' relationship, a child feels scared. The child looks at both faces and hears the tones in their voices. The child intuits something is wrong—someone is not OK—and maybe it's the child's fault. As Dr. Hiam Ginott says, "Children are like wet cement—whatever falls on them makes an impression."

Stress between parents at the top creates ten times more stress on the child at the bottom.

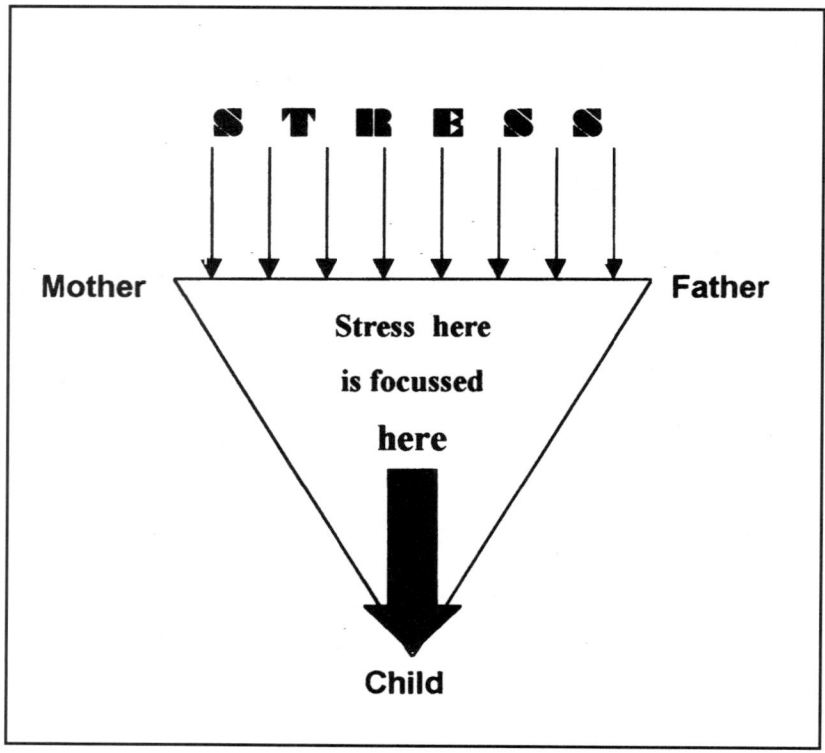

CONSCIOUS PARENTING 241

If one parent has the power and the other is subservient, which one is it safer for the child to identify with? The little child might decide to be a controller a persecutor, a victim or a rescuer. When a child finds his parents' relationship is stressful, the child frequently becomes a rescuer, with grandiose feelings of saving everybody (but himself). Sometimes he will feel unneeded (therefore unloved) by daddy, and needed desperately by mommy. The child thinks, "If I meet her needs, eventually she will be able to take care of me." In a healthy environment, children experience their parents loving each other and wanting and loving them, but not needing to be rescued in any way by the child.

Mary Pipher, Ph.D., in *The Shelter of Each Other: Rebuilding Our Families*, writes: "Human development occurs within the context of relationships. We learn from who we love."

We need to accept our children for who they are, not try to make them into who we wish they would become. If we think they are great, they will be great. Do you know why Jesus turned out so well? It is because his mother thought he was the Son of God!

"GOOD MORNING, MORTALS!"

©Ted Goff, Reprinted with Permission

Nick Stinett & John DeFrain in *The Secrets of Strong Families* say, "Strong families have roughly 20 positive comments for every negative one." Dr. Hiam Ginott says, "If you want children to improve, let them hear the nice things you say about them to others."

Accepting our children for who they are and seeing in them their potential for greatness, does not mean expecting them to be perfect. Let's not jail them in the prison of our expectations and control.

THE PRISON OF PARENTAL INFLUENCES

TRY HARD!
BE PERFECT!
BE NICE!
HURRY UP!

DON'T BE | DON'T BE YOU | DON'T BE CLOSE | DON'T BELONG | DON'T GROW UP | DON'T BE A CHILD | DON'T SUCCEED | DON'T BE WELL | DON'T BE SAFE | DON'T BE IMPORTANT

BE SWEET!
PLEASE ME!
BE STRONG!
BE CUTE!

WHO HAS THE KEY?

We need to see our children as an anthropologist would see a fascinating advanced culture—as beings who can teach us so much. We need to marvel at their words, study their unique habits, and stretch our minds and hearts to understand them, as we would communicate with an isolated being from a primitive yet spiritually advanced tribe. We need to learn to communicate in our children's terms—without imposing more adult structure than they're ready for.

We also need to be polite to our children. Remember to say, "Please," "Thank You," and "Excuse me." There is an old saying that is so cozy, "Treat your family like guests and your guests like family."

The first thing we need to do to take care of our children is to take care of ourselves. If we're healthy, happy, addiction-free, excited about life, and fulfilled in our careers, we can be good role models for our children, and refrain from pressuring them to live our unlived lives.

The three first steps in conscious parenting are:
• Heal your own childhood wounds.
• Live a balanced, healthy, happy, fulfilling life that models the life you wish for your child.
• Maintain a good, loving marriage.

Heal Your Own Childhood Wounds

Wounding gets passed on as a legacy. If we were emotionally burned as children, we pass the hot potato on to our children. Harville Hendrix says, "The single most important predictor of how you will parent is how you were parented as a child. The problems a parent has with a child relate directly to the problems her parents had with her when she was that age, and how they reacted to her."

We will automatically and unconsciously parent our children the way our parents parented us, or we will do the opposite in extreme—unless we heal our childhood wounds and relate to our children in ways that are best for them—not out of our frustrated past. We need to say to ourselves every day until we feel it in our cells, "He is not me. This is not my childhood. These are different times. This is now."

Doing the therapy to heal our childhood wounds is the best way to be good parents. I mean therapy that enables us to regress, be little again, make Redecisions, forgive our parents, and make closure with childhood. Just sitting around talking about today's daily problems without dealing with what it reminds you of from the past, won't do it.

In IMAGO therapy we use the Parent/Child Dialogue (explained in Chapter 3) to heal childhood wounds. Forgiving parents and all others from the past is the first step toward good parenting, so if you haven't already completed all the assignments in Chapter 10 to forgive all those from the past, go back and **forgive those parents**! They did the best they could considering the parenting they received, what they knew then, and the circumstances of their lives at the time.

Live a Balanced, Healthy, Happy, Fulfilling Life

Step 2 is to look at your life as the exact blueprint your children will follow. Is this what you want? We are all capable of change. Life is decisional, and you have the power to be the person you want your children to emulate. You are your children's role model. If you model healthy spiritual values, there is a greater chance your child will adopt some of the same values, or at least find his own healthy spiritual values. One of the ways we let our children down is to be too permissive, particularly with adolescents. As much as children hate it when we impose limits, they crave those limits. They are not yet capable of setting their own limits, and they need our guidance to show them how to do this.

In a recent article in Family Therapy Networker adapted from his book, *Nurturing Good Children Now*, psychologist Ron Taffel says, "Parents have become so anxious about not doing the *wrong* thing that they often become paralyzed." This leaves the child adrift, floating aimlessly in a sea of conflicting urges and temptations. It is often at this point that the child will turn to what Taffel calls the "second family—the kiddie culture of peers and media that is often more important, and more visible, than the 'first' families of their parents and siblings." The difficulty with the second family is that there are no moral guidelines which assist the child to find her way. Teenagers generally believe that "you only need to treat others the way they treat you."

The most direct route to helping a child feel understood is to treat him as an individual, not as an interchangeable 8-, 12-, or 16-year old. At the root of children's anger is the fear that no one really understands them. This makes them especially vulnerable to peer pressure, because their peers seem to be the only ones who truly do understand them. Most teachers are too busy and overworked to take the time to know each child, and many parents today are too preoccupied with earning a living and getting their own needs met to spend the time their children need them to devote to their upbringing.

Parents need to spend time with each child individually, and make that time a time of connection, instruction and guidance, always tempered with love and the awareness that everything is new to the child, and the mistakes they make are simply a part of learning. Learn to overlook those things your child does which do not seriously encroach on the important values and lessons you are trying to teach this child. Do everything you can to make this child feel unique and special. It takes a lot of direct, one-on-one time with a child to give that child the undivided attention he needs. When we take the time to get to know our child, spend quality time just being with our child, then we generate the closeness that helps the child respect us when we have to set limits and insist on outcomes which the child does not necessarily agree with. That respect can carry us through the difficult tasks of child raising with less angry fighting and more reluctant but genuine cooperation.

Maintain a Good, Loving Marriage

The most important way to teach your children love, in addition to loving them, is to live love in your marriage. Improving your marriage is a tremendous gift to your children. Reading this far in this book, you're already beginning to do that, so congratulate yourself!

STAGES OF CHILD DEVELOPMENT

Children grow through distinct stages of development, and if we know what to expect at each stage, we are better able to meet their needs. The most difficult stage for us as parents will often be the stage when our parents didn't meet our needs.

Birth through 18 months is the age of Attachment—parents need to be consistently available, warm and loving to the child. Babies need to see the love on their parents' faces, hear the happy tones in their voices, and feel the comfort of abundant skin touches. If a mother isn't nursing, she needs to sometimes hold the baby against her bare skin while she bottle feeds him to maximize the skin contact. Babies learn love through all their senses.

Babies also need alone time so they don't grow up with a low threshold of boredom. It's important to sometimes leave a baby alone to jabber to himself, explore his body, and notice objects around him. Among the many fad theories is one that teaches to be with your children constantly—asleep or awake. This seems unbalanced, and it deprives children of the experience of being comfortable alone—an experience all humans need.

18 to 36 months is the stage of Exploration—parents need to provide safety, support and encouragement for the child to explore his surroundings and be adventurous in his environment. From 36 months to 48 months is the stage of Identity—parents need to bestow approval and acceptance of all the many aspects of the child's developing personality.

Four to seven years is the stage of Competence—at this stage, parents need to provide guidance without force, and consistently praise the child's experimentation and learning. Seven to twelve years is the stage of Social Concerns—parents need to give support with flowing communication, to be emotionally available and generous in our praise, yet back off from being overly controlling. We need to give them the safety of firm rules, and still allow them to choose their own styles, friends, and hobbies without criticism.

Finally, from 12 to 18 years is the stage of Intimacy. At this stage more than any other it is important to role model healthy living. We need to exhibit consistent personal and family values. Communication without lecturing is more important than ever at this stage. We need to allow the child to differentiate and separate from us by "backing off." It is important to discuss our values about honesty, education, drugs, and sex openly, to tell them what we believe, and to walk our talk.

Children need discipline, just as they need food, water, sleep, play, approval, exploration, safety, and love. Parents who were raised too strictly sometimes follow outdated rules, causing the child to rebel from all authority. Sometimes parents rebel from their own strict upbringing by allowing their children to make their own rules. This can be very damaging to a child. The lack of limits not only confuses the child, it makes him feel unsafe. Often a child raised without parental rules learns that he can do anything he wants, without concern for the rights of others. Remember that the word discipline means to teach, not to punish. Don't be afraid to be the boss. Children are constantly testing, attempting to see how much they can get away with—how far you will let them go—and they secretly hope you will not let them go too far.

Children will test our limits to assure themselves that we care for them and will protect them from danger. When we maintain consistent and appropriate limits and values, they trust our love and eventually they internalize these limits so they can know right from wrong and build their own boundaries as they mature.

Disciplining is an important aspect of teaching boundaries and setting limits. The consequences need to fit the misbehavior. It is never OK to spank children, or to use physical violence for any reason. Spanking is the first step towards child abuse. Spanking teaches children to be physically abusive persecutors or helpless victims, especially when they become adults.

During a mother-daughter appointment the other day, I heard the intelligent mom say words to her teenage daughter that made my heart sing. She said, "I love you too much to be indifferent about your behavior."

We need to be firm in lovingly expressing our values to our children. The best way to start is, "I love you *and* I have expectations." It is important to let them know what our expectations are—about honesty, education, drugs, sex, alcohol, and responsibility. And remember—they learn ten times more from watching us than from listening to us. Our behavior is our most effective teaching tool. Let's remember to role model what we say, or our children will not believe us. James Baldwin wrote in *Nobody Knows My Name*, "Children have never been very good at listening to their elders, but they have never failed to imitate them."

I believe an important part of parenting is sharing nature with our children, exposing them to the natural world. There are children who think the mall is all there is. Mary Pipher, Ph.D., says in her book, *The Shelter of Each Other: Rebuilding Our Families*, "Children cannot love what they do not know. They cannot miss, what they have never experienced. Turn off the TV and computer for at least a couple of nights a week and talk to each other, and make sure that the family does something out of doors every week. Watch a sunset, go for a walk or take a trip to a wilderness area."

The natural world adds a spiritual dimension and promotes family bonding. When we experience the vastness of the ocean, the mountains, the fields, and the sky, we can more easily let go of our trivial complaints and connect with the larger picture.

The natural world has great power to heal and restore broken families. Family time out in nature is soul connecting, just as family time in shopping malls is disconnecting, harried, frequently produces arguments, and implies that buying things is what produces happiness. Children need contact with the natural world. It is an antidote to advertising and gives them a different perspective on the universe. Looking at the Milky Way makes most of us feel small and yet part of something vast. TV, with its emphasis on meeting every need, makes people feel self-important and yet unconnected to anything greater than themselves.

The negative ions in the air by the sea actually change our brain waves. In the mountains and on the tops of hills, we gain a higher perspective. Collecting shells or rocks together can help us to see beauty in nature, ourselves and each other, instead of only in material things. Gardening and growing things together enhances self-esteem. Start sharing nature with children when they are young, and make great outdoor adventures regular rituals—whether they're daily, weekly, monthly or annual vacations. Then your children are more likely to find solace in nature rather than drugs or alcohol, and they will always remember the happy times of childhood. The great outdoors speaks to the heart, gives meaning to lives and produces authentic soul unfoldment.

Now about those teenage years! If you can survive them with more pleasure than pain, and more pride and calm than worry and anger, you are on the path of transformation! As Rebecca Richards says, "Oh, to be only half as wonderful as my child thought I was when he was small, and only half as stupid as my teenager now thinks I am." Mary Pipher, Ph.D. says, "Raising teenagers is not for the faint of heart."

Often couples have been confused about when it is healthy to divorce. I believe that we have been too ready to divorce; the tools and exercises in this book are designed to help couples to deal with their difficulties so they can and will stay together. I encourage couples who have children to do everything they can to stay married. You have a responsibility to your children to provide them the stability of a family. Divorce when children are young is devastating for them. It can affect everything from their educational achievement to their intimate relationships to their lifetime earning ability, and many children of divorce have scars that don't heal.

In *The Unexpected Legacy of Divorce*, Judith Wallerstein followed 93 children of failed marriages over a 25 year period. She concludes that children of divorced parents have more difficulty establishing intimate relationships in adult years, are less likely to go to college, and more likely to have problems with drugs and alcohol. In other words, the effects of divorce on children last long into adulthood.

Dr. Alvin Poussaint, a psychiatry professor at Harvard Medical School who also consults on family-oriented TV programs, says, "Couples should weigh the contributions each makes to the family, rather than making a decision based on circumstances one spouse might face.

Pepper Schwartz, a sociology professor at the University of Washington, who specializes in marriage and family issues, says the phase "for better or worse should not be taken literally. If they've got at least a 50-50 good-bad ratio and it works for both parties and there's not a lot of conflict, then staying married for children might have some merit—provided the parents still respect each other. But if people are actively unhappy and they don't raise their children together, then I think those people have a life as much as those kids do."

Most therapists agree that the loss of romantic love is less important than the children. "The children don't care if you're in love," says Frank Pittman, an Atlanta family therapist who wrote the best-seller, *Private Lies: Infidelity and the Betrayal of Intimacy*. "You don't have to be in love to be loving."

When you have children growing up and you both love them, you need to do everything you can to learn to live together in harmony. The first step can be to read this book together and do all the exercises faithfully. The second step would be to go together to psychotherapists ***who specialize in couple therapy***, especially IMAGO therapists or PAIRS® therapists.

The most loving thing you can do for your children next to loving them is to provide them with a two parent harmonious home. If you are a couple with children and you are considering divorce, I strongly recommend that you both attend at least one year of weekly therapy before you make any decision regarding divorce.

Thomas Moore, author of *Care of the Soul* and *The Re-Enchantment of Everyday Life,* says: "As a society, we could allow children a lot more presence than we do, and let children influence the way we design our society. I think as it is, the children are greatly repressed. We have many ways of repressing children, especially through our schooling system. If we lived as many cultures in this world today do, where the children have more presence and therefore influence the structure, we would change, and I think we would find enchantment... If you see the way people live on a Saturday night any other place in the world, you could go to the city square and find families out, all different ages and types. That creates a different world. The so-called third world that we think is poor, is really rich in things like this."

Dr. Jane M. Healy says in *How To Be An Authoritative Parent Not An Authoritarian One*:

"Being a good parent is not as difficult or mysterious as it may seem. Sure, there are times when parents find themselves yelling at their children...other times when they know they're giving in too easily...still other times when they actually feel they might be doing it right."

THE THREE PARENTAL TYPES

Child-development experts have been researching the topic of parenting for several decades and have identified three basic styles:

Permissive

These parents are quick to give in to a child's demands and allow him more freedom than he may be ready for. Permissive parents may even allow a small child to make important decisions that should be the adults' responsibility — such as which nursery school he will attend.

Reason: Some permissive parents simply don't care enough to make appropriate demands on their child. Others don't really know any better. And some, in a well-meaning attempt to encourage the child's self-expression and democracy, go too far, so that the child winds up running the household. The result of permissive parenting may be a child who pushes his limits or never learns the meaning of self-control, acting up until a parent or teacher finally comes down on him—hard.

Authoritarian

At the other extreme are *authoritarian* parents who make arbitrary or inflexible rules that leave no room for negotiation. The child is expected to conform to the parents' image in everything from behavior and appearance to after school activities and, eventually, career choice. If the child falls short, he's punished—either physically or psychologically, through the threat of losing the parents love, or both.

Authoritative

Authoritative parents have the most well-adjusted children and the most satisfying relationships with them. Unlike authoritarian or permissive parents, authoritative parents are flexible and structured. They're highly involved with and observant of their children. And their kids respect them, as well. Anyone who sincerely wants to be a better parent can learn to practice the basic elements of authoritative parenting.

RESPONSIVENESS

• **Authoritative parents are sensitive to their children.** They listen carefully and hear and acknowledge the child's point of view. They express genuine interest in what their children are doing: "It sounds as if you're really enjoying that project in science class." They notice the child's emotional state: "You look kind of down—did you have a not-so-good day?"
• **They show warmth and affection.** Authoritative parents are quick to hug, express delight and tell their children how much they enjoy their company.
• **Authoritative parents acknowledge their**

children's accomplishments in specific and encouraging ways:** "You really learned a lot from writing that paper...Congratulations on learning to skate backwards—that's hard to do."
- **They notice that children's needs change as they get older.** Authoritative parents don't expect the approach that worked with a five-year-old to be effective for an eight-year-old. They read books on development, talk to other parents and observe other children as well as their own.
- **Authoritative parents reason and communicate openly with their children.** They don't keep a lot of secrets—and their children know they can trust their parents to tell the truth. That doesn't mean revealing the contents of the family bank book, but it does mean taking the children's interest seriously: "The family finances are something we don't discuss with you kids yet, but don't worry there's enough money for us to have a very nice life together."

STRUCTURE

- **Authoritative parents make appropriate demands for mature behavior.** A three-year-old should certainly be dressing and feeding himself, but can't be expected to sit through a long lecture on good manners. Parents can encourage appropriate challenges by arranging the environment so that the child's efforts are supported.

   Example: A parent and a toddler are playing with blocks.

   The ***permissive*** parent might leave the child alone to push the blocks around aimlessly or throw them.

   The ***authoritarian*** parent might point to the picture on the box and say, "Build a tower like this one."

   The ***authoritative*** parent might put three blocks on top of each other and say, "Look I'm building a tower,"

encouraging the child to add another block.
- **Authoritative parents establish and enforce consistent, age-appropriate rules.** Any parent will fly off the handle once in a while, but she understands that the most powerful enforcement is gentle yet firm—and strives for that. Effective reminders include, "We agreed that"—"I expect you to"—"The rule is." Negotiation within the limits you've set is important. Children should have the freedom to meet your expectations *in their own ways.*

Example: The child insists that he do his homework with music playing. The ***authoritarian*** parent might say, "Absolutely not. Turn that trash off now."

The ***permissive*** parent might say, "Whatever you want to do."

The ***authoritative*** parent might say, "Let's try one week with music and one week without. If your homework doesn't suffer, you can have music...but keep it quiet and in your own room."
- **They keep instructions simple.** It is too much for a five-year-old to keep track of the following: "You left the bathroom a mess. Run upstairs and straighten it out, then get your things together so we can go to the store."

Better: "First, put all your dirty towels in the hamper. Second, bring your coat downstairs so we can go out."

OPTIMUM CONTROL

- **Authoritative parents maintain a degree of control over their children.** They don't let them run wild, but they avoid being arbitrary ("I don't like that sport, so you're not going to play it"), restrictive ("No friends over this week—you have too much homework"), or overly punitive ("You're grounded for six months"). They promote understanding rather than compliance.

Example: Instead of saying to your ten-year-old, "Forget community theater tryouts—you're enrolling in summer school," you might sit down with him and say, "You obviously have a lot of options this summer. What are some of the things you've thought about doing?"

He might mention the play, a summer job, and the fact that his English teacher thinks he needs to take a summer-school writing course. Your response, "What are some of the reasons for doing each of these things?" After talking it through, you might observe, "Right now the play sounds like more fun, but can you see why taking the English course might be better?" If he absolutely refuses, at some point the choice is his—and he'll have to deal with the consequence of struggling through high school English. You could force him into summer school, but he's likely to be so resentful that he won't get anything out of the class.

Probably the hardest thing about being a parent is relinquishing enough control so that children can make their own mistakes—and learn from them. If parents let their children make the *little* mistakes while they're little people, they'll be much less likely to make *big* mistakes when they're big people.

"OK, I CAN WALK AND TALK NOW, SO I'LL JUST BE ON MY WAY. THANKS FOR ALL THE BANANAS!"

© Ted Goff, Reprinted with Permission

USE THE FOLLOWING EXAMPLE TO HELP GUIDE THE DEVELOPMENT OF A HEALTHY SENSE OF RESPONSIBILITY

Age	Freedom	Limits
Under 5 Parent provides structure, safety limits and rules.	May go outside Choose breakfast Watch television	Stay inside the fence Cold or hot cereal *Sesame Street, Mr. Rogers.*
Between 5 & 7 Parent gives more opportunities for independence & other responsibilities.	Choose what to wear. Select hobbies & activities.	This rack for school, this rack for play. If they are respectful to self & if we can afford them.
Between 8-12 Parent begins teaching drug & alcohol prevention, the best time, being after fully developed thinking & before puberty.	Select time for homework. Select a way to contribute to the family. Decide when to do chores.	After school, before or after dinner From a job list, or in a way that the family agrees to. Before dinner or before bedtime.
Over 13 Parent continues encouraging sufficiency & connection with adult world of responsibility.	Choose bedtime. Get driver's license. Borrow family car.	Be in your bedroom by... No late showers or loud music after 10 PM on school nights. After satisfactory arrangements are made for insurance. If arranged beforehand & gas is replaced. No drinking or drugs.

More than anything, children need to connect—with you! When they act in negative or destructive ways, it's usually because they haven't learned a positive way to get your time and attention. All children crave attention, approval and love, and will act in negative ways for attention if they're not receiving enough strokes. The most important elements of conscious parenting are:
• To be healed from your own childhood wounds.
• To be happy in your adult relationships.
• To communicate regularly, and more important, to listen, to stretch to understand what your child is trying to tell you.
• To understand each stage of development, and to provide safety by setting appropriate limits.
• To lavish positive strokes—verbal (compliments and praise) and nonverbal (smiles and hugs)—upon him.

Many years ago, Mark Twain said, "We are always too busy for our children; we never give them the time or interest they deserve. We lavish gifts upon them; but the most precious gift—our personal association, which means so much to them—we give grudgingly."

Two of the best new books on parenting are *Giving the Love that Heals: A Guide for Parents*, by Harville Hendrix and Helen Hunt, and *The Five Love Languages of Children*, by Gary Chapman & Ross Campbell, M.D.

KIDS WHO ARE DIFFERENT

Here's to the kids who are different,
The kids who don't always get A's,
The kids who have ears twice the size of their peers,
And noses that go on for days...
Here's to the kids who are different,
The kids they call crazy or dumb,
The kids who don't fit, with the guts and the grit,
Who dance to a different drum.
Here's to the kids who are different,
The kids with the mischievous streak,
For when they have grown, as history's shown,
It's their difference that makes them unique.
—Digby Wofe

There are children in Bosnia and Croatia and in so many other places in the world who are suffering. I would like to share this prayer with you. The author is anonymous:

We pray for children
   Who sneak popsicles before supper.
   Who erase holes in math workbooks.
   Who can never find their shoes.
And we pray for those
   Who stare at photographers from behind barbed wire,
   Who can't bound down the street in a new
      pair of sneakers,
Who never "counted potatoes,"
Who are born in places we wouldn't be caught
   dead in,
Who never saw a circus,
Who live in an X-rated world.
We pray for children
   Who bring us sticky kisses and fistfuls of
      dandelions,
   Who hug us in a hurry and forget their

lunch money.
And we pray for those
   Who never get dessert,
   Who have no security blanket to drag
         behind them,
   Who watch their parents watch them die,
   Who can't find any bread to steal,
   Who don't have any rooms to clean up,
   Whose pictures aren't on anybody's dresser,
   Whose monsters are real.
We pray for children
   Who spend all their allowance before Tuesday,
   Who throw tantrums in the grocery store
         and pick at their food,
   Who like ghost stories,
   Who shove their dirty clothes under the bed
         and never rinse out the tub,
   Who get visits from the tooth fairy,
   Who don't like to be kissed in front of
         the carpool,
   Who squirm in church or temple and scream
         into the phone,
   Whose tears we sometimes laugh at
   And whose smiles can make us cry.
And we pray for those
   Whose nightmares come in the daytime,
   Who will eat anything,
   Who have never seen a dentist,
   Who aren't spoiled by anybody,
   Who go to bed hungry and cry themselves
         to sleep,
   Who live and move, but have no being.
We pray for children who want to be carried,
   And for those who must be.
   For those we never give up on,
   And for those who never get a second chance.
   For those we smother
   And for those who will grab the hand of
         anybody kind enough to offer it.

—Notes—

—Notes—

14
Back to the Beginning—Living Together

"To get the full value of joy, you must have someone to divide it with."
—Mark Twain

Rick: I mean, what am I supposed to call you? My "Girl Friend"? My "Companion"? My "Roommate"? Nothing sounds quite right!
Joanie: How about your "Reason for Living"?
Rick: No, no. I need something I can use around the office.
—from *Doonesbury*, by Garry Trudeau

THERE FOR ME

> You are there for me
>   when I need you
> Whether I want you there
>   or not
> To push me
>   when I want to drop out
> To confront me
>   when I want to cop out
> To cook a healthy meal
>   when I'd just eat out
> To hold me
>   when I'm full of doubt
> To bring a smile
>   when I'd rather pout.
> At night you open yourself to me
> Your arms spread to catch me
>   as I fall into love.
> Your heart enfolds me
>   as I come home.
>   —John Tyler

Are you unsure about giving up your so-called freedom and settling down with one person? Are you telling yourself that "variety is the spice of life"? Well, Dear Wonderer, I have some adult information for you: if you organize your life in a sequence of short delights with people interchangeably chosen to help you make better love to yourself, you will find before very long that you've used yourself up. You will numb your capacity for long lasting, conscious love. Eleanor Roosevelt said, "One's philosophy is not best expressed in words. It is expressed in the choices one makes...the process never ends until we die. And the choices we make are ultimately our responsibility."

Living together as a preamble to marriage is a

BACK TO THE BEGINNING—LIVING TOGETHER

relatively new concept, practiced widely in this and the last generation; in our grandparents' day, it was unheard of. We each need to figure out for ourselves what is right and what is good *for us*, and not rely on old or inherited ideas.

For some couples, living together is a brilliant way to find out if this truly is the person with whom to share life's journey. It is also a companionable, easier and more fun way to live while you are making wedding plans and sharing chores, expenses, companionship, and laughs. Sharing a home together adds richness and texture to your lives. In the cradle of the home we make and care for together, we can soften and transform our lives.

People used to marry and then move in together. Civilization moves forward. So many smart young and not-so-young couples live together as a practice hall and learn things they would never learn any other way. Several living-together couples have done therapy with us and then asked us to officiate at their wedding at the end of the training. How convenient to work through the Power Struggle Stage and the Learning and Transformational Stage while you are exposed to each other's irritating and endearing daily habits. How astonishing it can be to extravagantly observe your dream man or woman in your own oasis. At such close range, with such profound sharing and no secrets, your relationship can grow into full Into-me-see.

So many people have come to our PAIRS® Training or therapy sessions undecided about whether to move in together. In many cases we suggest this test:
• Do you love this person more than you have ever loved anyone before?
• Do you feel loved, cherished and even better about yourself when you are with him?
• Are you proud of him?
• Do you admire and respect him?
• Have you known each other well for at least six months to a year?

- Are you both free of drugs, alcohol and other addictions?
- Do you trust him 100 percent and feel safe in the relationship?
- Can you happily imagine having children together and growing old together?
- Have you had differences you have been able to work through?
- Are you equals or is one a Victim (financially or emotionally) and the other a Rescuer?
- Do you share responsibilities equally?
- Are you both free of verbal and physical abuse?
- Do you have similar values?
- Are your relationship patterns stable, with neither of you having had many short relationships and marriages with left-over unfinished business?
- Are you both willing to seek Couple Therapy when extreme anger, scare or withdrawal arises?
- Do you both agree to be monogamous?
- Do you individually feel like you are soul mates?

Edward Sellner says, "A soul mate is someone with whom we can share our greatest joys and deepest fears, confess our worst sins and most persistent faults, clarify our highest hopes and perhaps most unarticulated dream."

If you answer yes to all of these questions, you can decide now to be a risk taker. Take up what you have and walk together. You have a partner, you have love, and you have the present. That is enough to begin.

I strongly advise couples moving in together to draw up contracts, house guidelines and relationship rules. Oh, the arguments written agreements avoid! If you want help with contracting, take a vacation to Maui and we will help you make your contract in Paradise.

So many people do not leave their partner, but they spend energy wondering if they should for the rest of their lives. Consequently, they will have no real life. I invite you to decide now to let what is meaningless be meaningless, and courageously make the commitment! Live to-

It's not you, Rob. It's just that things are moving a little too fast.

The New Yorker Collection, 1993, Peter Steiner from cartoonbank.com. All Rights Reserved.

gether, then marry—or marry and live together simultaneously. Consider your situation and your partner's situation, and know that one definition of courage is being afraid and doing it anyway.

Shared pain is half the pain, and shared joy is double joy.

HAPPILY MARRIED FOREVER

"But you can't leave, Helen—I still have so much to learn from women."

The New Yorker Collection, 1992, Lee Lorenz
from cartoonbank.com. All Rights Reserved.

©Nicole Hollander, Reprinted with Permission

BACK TO THE BEGINNING—LIVING TOGETHER 269

"If we're running away from love because of a feeling of unworthiness, then we need to stop and remember who we are: children of the Creator, sons and daughters of the Light, rightful heirs to all the love and power of the universe." —Barry and Joyce Vissell

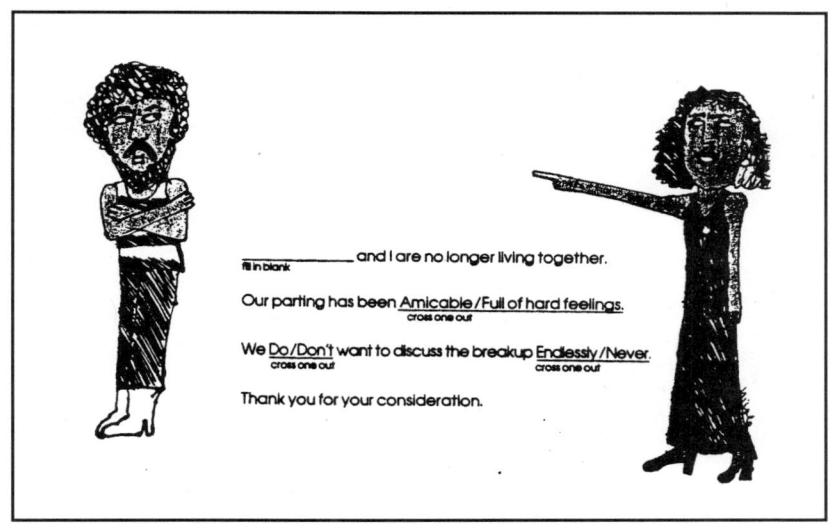

©Nicole Hollander. Reprinted with Permission.

—Notes—

15

Marriage Commitment

"And then I asked him with my eyes to ask again yes and then he asked me would I yes...and his heart was going like mad and yes I said yes I will YES."
—James Joyce

IN ME

There's no place in me
that I can go
where you aren't there.

I can plumb the depths
of my being
and there is always you.

As deep as I go
I cannot get to a place
where there's just me.
—John Tyler

"When the energies of romantic passion are contained and stabilized by commitment and discipline, marriage becomes an emotional bond and a transformative process equal to any other structure for personal growth yet devised by human beings—including psychotherapy and religion." —Harville Hendrix

Commitment is inherent in any genuinely loving relationship. Anyone who is truly concerned for the spiritual growth of another knows, consciously and instinctively, that he can significantly foster growth only through a relationship of constancy. Couples cannot resolve in any healthy way the universal issues of marriage—dependence and independence, dominance & submission, freedom and fidelity, power and control—without the security of knowing that the act of struggling over these issues will not in itself destroy the relationship.

Stephen Levine says, "The power of commitment to only one in a monogamous relationship intensifies the power of commitment to one's own growth, maturity and enlightenment, and to the One and Only. The resolve to merge solely with one other fuels the practice of self-discovery and healing."

Marriage is not only a discipline for the good life, but a spiritual journey. The commitment to marriage means two people have chosen each other to love, to nourish, to forgive, to heal, to make safe, to share passion, to support, and to act with intention. Each needs the other's input and cooperation to develop the art of living well. M. Scott Peck says, "Commitment is the foundation, the bedrock of any genuinely loving relationship."

Marriage means I commit to share my life with you through challenges, changes, trials, grief, pain, and *joy*. John and I have a "no leave" clause in our marriage contract. If we at any time have such strong disagreements or differences that we cannot work them through

MARRIAGE COMMITMENT

alone, we agree to go to marriage specialists for therapy for as long as six years to work through to the next spiritual level of our life-long journey together.

Reprinted with special permission
from King Features Syndicate

If that surprises you, maybe you do not know how much fun therapy can be. We have people who come to therapy for five, eight, and even ten years for continual coaching to help them grow to a higher place in their development. These are some of the healthiest, happiest, most fun, and easy to be with people we have ever met. They are all in loving, conscious relationships now, and had a rollicking good time getting there. It is better than divorcing and making the same mistakes over and over with different people, or growing old alone.

Marriage is a practical and enjoyable way to grow up, to gain a live-in Guru, a life teacher, and a mirror to see your whole self more fully. After dating or living together, a commitment to marry will change your life in unexpected and profound ways. Commitment adds the necessary ingredient of safety to the passion you are already experiencing. You will experience deeper and more profound intimacy after you marry, and even more as you progress through each stage of your marriage.

Couples who have achieved glowing personal fulfillment in their marriage during many years of Deep Vintage Love can relate to the world with the same sense of mutual responsibility, creativity and responsiveness that they have learned by practicing with each other all those years. Some happy co-creative couples even volunteer together for causes they strongly believe in. Some find their marriages so satisfying they start businesses together so they can synergize their talents, and rejoice in seeing each other twenty-four hours a day. The man who brings me freshly squeezed orange juice in bed on Sunday mornings, works with me, writes poems with me, cooks with me, and shares new ideas while showering, beach walking, eating and sky watching. We are never bored with each other, and at this rate we will still be passionate lovers at age 101 (our plan.)

"The two of you are reflections of each other, the One God masquerading as two bodies, two minds, two hearts, perfectly complimentary to each other."
—Joyce and Barry Vissell

MARRIAGE COMMITMENT

—Notes—

16

Blended Families

"Choose to be right or kind."
—Tagore

Once upon a time there was a very happy woman who was ecstatically in love. She had finally met the man of her dreams. After a long unhappy marriage, a short rebound tryst, and then some lonely years, she was finally with the great love of her life. Nothing could go wrong or cause dissention as they made their life plans.

The woman in love had dreams of being the perfect stepmother. She had always wanted a large family, and she thought it would be easy. She thought of herself as warm and generous—many interim divorced men had courted her, partly because they thought she would make "such a good stepmother for my kids, because you're so fun-loving, natural and nurturing with young people." And she was eager to give her only daughter some sisters (she already had three brothers) for some cozy family blending.

Then she met his youngest daughter, who had lived with her mother after the divorce. At their first meeting, the young girl said, "I always thought my father and mother would get back together, and I still think they would if it weren't for you." The happy woman in love suddenly forgot everything she had read about being a stepmother. She became defensive, and said, "Your parents have been divorced for ten years, and your mother's been re-married and divorced since then!"

The young girl countered with, "He's never dated

anyone or spent time with any women, so I didn't think he'd ever marry anyone." The insulted woman, who thought the children would be happy to see their father so happy with her, said, "But he's dated so many women, and he had such a close relationship with one." The "antagonist" retreated to, "I don't believe you." That was the beginning of our client's "so-called" life as a stepparent!

Divorce is a traumatic experience for children—some never recover—and it always leaves deep scars. Some children stay emotionally stuck at the age they were when their parents divorced. When you meet someone new, it is important to tell your children soon about your new friendship. As you grow in love, it is even more important to tell the children. When you decide to marry, be sure to include them in your wedding plans.

As stepmother, first seek to become friends and spend time with the children; hold back your mother love, and don't overwhelm them or try to compete with their biological mother. Honor each other's family customs, be flexible, and remember that children of divorce probably have unhealed wounds. A stepmother needs to remember that it is not about her when the children criticize her, compare her, or are cool to her. It is about *their* hurts and disappointments.

Sometimes it takes years for a family to blend smoothly after being roughed up in the fast, noisy, chaotic blender of divorce. The children may have experienced two parents with vastly different life styles and values. They may have overheard uncomplimentary opinions about the other parent or new stepparent from their jealous mother or father, or worse, one parent may have actually said uncomplimentary things about the other to the children. Sometimes a lonely, guilt-ridden, divorced parent will spend vast amounts of time and money on his children, and then remarry. Now some of his time and money is spent on his new wife and their life together, and this can cause resentment from his children toward the new wife.

It's best to let the father handle this. He should be the one to explain to his children that he wants to share his life with a partner, and he is glad not to be lonely any longer. It is important for him to reassure the children that he loves them just as much, but he never intended to stay single for the rest of his life, and that parents can't get all their needs met by their children. How much to explain about that and about money depends on the ages of the children.

There is so much involved in the healthy blending of families. It takes honesty, a vast amount of love, and years of shared good times. The stepparent needs to step back and not *expect* to be loved, and to resist competing with the child's other parent—the ex-spouse. Don't expect or ask the child to call you "Mom" or "Dad". They already have a Mom or a Dad, and you're not it. Find another term they can call you that you like too.

This book is mostly about couple relationships. There are many books on the market about blended families, so this chapter is necessarily short, because it would take a whole book to do justice to this important subject. I urge all divorced parents to read and *study* some of these books on step-parenting and blending families, particularly Drescher (1986) and Lofax (1995), before taking the drastic and generous step of living together.

Just one word of advice: one more way to become closer in marriage is to be a wonderful step-parent to your spouse's children. Every day when I count my blessings, I include deep gratitude to my husband for being such a loving step-dad and step-grandparent to our kids and grandkids.

—Notes—

Epilogue

Until we can laugh at our tragedies, we have not fully processed the experience. Until we can cry at other people's tragedies, we have not joined the human race. We all have our stories. Part of healing is to give up the familiar, self-limiting tales we tell ourselves, and embrace other possibilities.

WORDS OF THE WISE

"Foolish selfish people are always thinking of themselves, and the result is negative. Wise selfish people think of others, help others as much as they can, and the result is that they too reap some benefits. This is my simple religion. There is no need for temples, no need for complicated philosophy. Our own brain, our own heart, is the temple, the philosophy is kindness."
—The Dalai Lama

"To become who you are, you must see yourself in another yourself who is better able to manifest yourself than you are. This other self could be the sun or snowflakes or crystal clear water trickling from its source."
— Pir Vilayat Inayat Khan

"We are all waiting for the Messiah. But we decide if we will wait in misery, or wait in joy."
—Rabbi Joseph Gelberman

"Rule your mind or it will rule you."—Horace

"Happiness, or misery, is in the mind. It is the mind that lives."—William Corbett

"Mind moves matter."—Virgil

"True contentment depends not upon what we have. A tub was large enough for Diogenes, but a world was too little for Alexander."—C.C. Colton

©Edgar Argo, Reprinted with Permission

"The mind is its own place, and in itself can make a heaven of hell, a hell of heaven."—John Milton

"I decided that I would make my life my argument. I would advocate the things I believed in, in terms of the nine lives and what I did."—Albert Schweitzer

EPILOGUE

"I want to be thoroughly used up when I die, for the harder I work the more I love. I rejoice in life for its own sake. Life is no brief candle to me. It is a sort of splendid torch which I have gotten a hold of for a moment, and I want to make it burn as brightly as possible before handing it on to future generations."—George B. Shaw

"Some men see things as they are and say why ... I dream things that never were, and say why not."
—Robert Kennedy

"I love what I am doing. My only advice is to fall in love with your future. That is what I have always done, and it works."—George Burns

"Success is a process, a quality of mind and way of being, an outgoing affirmation of life."—Alex Noble

"I believe that genius is an infinite capacity for taking life by the scruff of the neck."—Christopher Quill

"Here is the test to find whether your mission on earth is finished: if you're alive, it isn't."—Richard Bach

"I have been all things unholy. If God can work through me he can work through anyone."
—Author unknown

"Great is the art of beginning, but greater is the art of ending."—Henry Wadsworth Longfellow

—Notes—

Appendix A

A HEALTHY HAPPY PERSON IS SOMEONE WHO

• Respects and loves her body, knows when her body needs something (food, air, water, rest) and does what she needs to get it.
• Keeps clean and dresses cleanly and neatly.
• Eats regular healthy, nutritious, attractively prepared meals.
• Exercises regularly and gets enough fresh air and sunshine.
• Enjoys her body in some or any of the following ways: bubble baths, hot tubs, massages, self massages with good smelling good feeling lotion, regular hugs with friends, partners, children, co-workers or therapists, caressing and kissing with lover, regular bonding and good sex.
• Makes sure the environment supports her physical needs by living in a clean, neat, aesthetically pleasing home.
• Refrains from taking *any* nicotine or hard drugs; puts a minimum of additives in her system; and does not take alcohol, coffee or marijuana on a regular or habitual basis.
• Is free of psychosomatic symptoms.
• Sleeps well without medication.
• Is free of addictions—alcohol, cigarettes, marijuana, sugar, chocolate, coffee, TV, workaholism, addictive relationships, anger, sadness, obsessing about the past, fantasy life, co-dependency, sleeping pills, drugs. An addiction is anything you feel tempted to lie about, anything you are defensive about, anything you are not willing to give up, or anything that keeps you unaware of what is going on around you. Something you do in moderation

when you choose at appropriate times is probably not an addiction.
- Does not display habitual, automatic, robotic behavior.
- Feels feelings fully and goes underneath any former addiction to discover his own creativity, blocked energy, and very life affirming essence.
- Is free of phobias (unreasonable, panicky fears).
- Lives in the HERE AND NOW, and doesn't spend time feeling guilty or angry about the past or worrying about the future.
- Has removed parent masks from authority figures, friends and lovers, and has forgiven parents, former friends, lovers and herself, has made closure and let go of the past.
- Knows the difference between reality and fantasy
- Knows what he feels and thinks and can recognize and acknowledge other people's feelings.
- Knows and keeps boundaries between himself and others.
- Has the ability to find out what others think and feel when he does not know.
- Does not automatically take on the thoughts and feelings of others.
- Separates thoughts and feelings from actions.
- Allows himself to cry when appropriate, and is willing to feel sadness and grief when he has to let go of something that was important to him.
- Recognizes and expresses anger, resentments and frustrations clearly and promptly when he feels them, and doesn't save stamps and let them build up.
- Forgives others and himself easily (allows 10 minutes for anger and then lets go). If it takes longer than 10 minutes, it's rubber banding back to the past—usually childhood.
- Recognizes and communicates the reasons for his values and beliefs.
- Recognizes and understands that others have different

reasons for their values and beliefs.
- Is comfortable sharing his ideas and opinions with others who have ideas of their own, even if their ideas are different.
- Confronts others when he has problems with what they are doing, saying or feeling.
- Is vocal and stubborn in opposing things he feels are destructive.
- Sometimes spends time with people more knowledgeable than himself.
- Knows that what she reads and how she treats others is more important than making a fashion statement, spending time in beauty salons, and pursuing liposuction and face lifts.
- Knows what he wants and talks straight and asks lovingly and assertively for what he wants and needs in all situations.
- Says "yes" and "no" straight.
- Knows the difference between wants and needs.
- Takes care of his own wants and needs and pleases himself without hurting others.
- Is comfortable negotiating openly with others to satisfy his needs and wants.
- Makes his own decisions.
- Is comfortable asking questions when he doesn't understand or wants to know something.
- Is comfortable learning how to do new things and can enjoy himself by exploring something new.
- Tries new things without getting in trouble or hurting himself.
- Knows when to take risks—can feel scared and do it anyway.
- Knows the difference between excitement and danger, and protects himself from real danger.
- Knows when to give up on something that is not working.
- Sometimes changes his mind. Intelligent people are

glad to have new information. Our only real loyalty is to Truth, not our own prejudices.
• Remembers that no two things are ever the same—each individual within a group is different from the others.
• Knows that no one thing remains the same for very long. Heraclitus said, "You can't step into the same river twice." A river, like every aspect of life, is a moving band of constant change. When we recognize this basic truth, we become more reasonable and less dogmatic.
• Rethinks religion & beliefs. True intelligence demands that we consider the separate components of our faith, one by one.
• Makes plans, decisions and agreements easily, carries them through to completion, and is responsible.
• Does things as well as they need to be done without feeling compelled to do perfect work or to be perfect.
• Finishes things that need to be finished.
• Uses all his potential and functions well in a fulfilling, healthy, honest main activity (school or work).
• If not in school, financially supports himself without hassles or excessive debt, and is realistic about money.
• Has fun every day, laughs regularly, feels "free child" enthusiasm and excitement—can look at a sunset and say, "Wow!"
• Feels good 85% of the time.
• Is able to enjoy sex fully and experience orgasms.
• Gives and accepts strokes (compliments) easily and honestly.
• Is able and willing to nurture himself and others.
• Enjoys his own company and is not afraid of being alone. Thomas Merton said, "Not all people are called to be hermits, but all people need enough silence and solitude in their lives to enable the deep inner voice of their own true self to be heard at least occasionally."
• Enjoys the company of others, and accepts and encourages intimacy without withdrawing.
• Knows how to negotiate and contract for private time for

himself and his partner (to read, think, imagine and meditate) without feeling abandoned.
- Recognizes and is comfortable with the fact that he is connected to other people.
- Is interdependent with others without sacrificing his autonomy.
- Does not have to be right or need to change intimate others so they believe and act as he wants them to.
- Trusts himself and others and checks out paranoid feelings and asks instead of reading people's minds.
- Takes full responsibility for every aspect of his life, including his actions, words, feelings and the people he chooses to bring into his life.
- Takes responsibility for his mistakes and his behavior, and says, "I'm sorry. I won't do that again" or "I'd like to learn a better way," instead of being defensive.
- Does not look for other people or circumstances to blame.
- Finds and accepts the lessons in mistakes, rejects guilt from the past, and moves on using the gifts.
- Keeps growing and learning new things, and is willing to change archaic attitudes or actions that no longer work.
- Knows when to seek outside help and is willing to ask for it.
- Knows how to choose trained experts—therapists, doctors, dentists, chiropractors, acupuncturists, teachers, lawyers and mechanics, or whatever resources are needed.
- Knows how to use these resources wisely and without games.
- Believes "I'm O.K, you're O.K."
- Avoids the DRAMA TRIANGLE (described in Chapter 2).

Appendix B

PARENTING EXERCISES

Here is our list of what a Happy, Healthy Family is like:

A HEALTHY, HAPPY FAMILY IS ONE IN WHICH

- Parents and children respect each other as people, are friendly and accept each other as they are, and don't criticize or expect anyone to "be perfect."
- Parents and children respect each other's privacy.
- Parents do not compare children with each other or with anyone else.
- Parents can disagree and argue openly and negotiate and forgive each other and the children.
- Parents and children express anger in healthy ways and let go of anger after ten minutes.
- The family goes to a school counselor or psychotherapist when there are differences which "cannot" be settled.
- Parents don't withdraw from each other or the children.
- There is open and frequent verbal and physical affection between all family members. Parents hug and kiss each other and the children daily, especially when someone leaves or comes home.
- Parents give and get strokes freely from each other and the children, and encourage children to do the same.
- Parents take an interest in children's school, jobs and extra-curricular activities.
- Each family member is encouraged to take responsibility for mistakes.
- Parents recognize that children learn from mistakes and blame is minimal. "The only thing I'll ever get mad at you for is when you do something you know is wrong."
- Parents set boundaries and limits, make family rules, and conduct family meetings or at least family talks

when issues arise.
- Parents discipline children in appropriate ways and always with love and support; punishment is not severe and fits the problem.
- Parents teach children how to manage pain and stress.
- Parents take care of children, nurture and accept and love them unconditionally.
- Parents do not ask children to advise them or take care of them.
- Children have allowances and do chores appropriate for their age, but have ample free time to do school work and play.
- Children do not take over parent roles and are not forced to take care of or play with younger siblings, or to stay home from school to do adult housework.
- Parents do not use children as confidantes to complain about the other parent.
- Parents do not pressure children to think and feel as they do.
- Parents encourage children to think their own thoughts and feel their own feelings.
- There are no "family secrets"—family circumstances which are ignored or not discussed.
- Parents encourage children to ask for advice and then make their own decisions.
- Parents bring up children to be autonomous people, so that by ages 18-21, the children can make their own decisions. By the time a child has graduated from college they no longer need financial support from parents.
- Parents encourage children to grow up, and do not manipulate them to keep them in symbiosis or dependency to meet the parent's needs.
- Parents encourage children to make their own friends, and accept the children's friends without judgment unless they are seriously disturbed, in which case the family talks it over fairly.
- Children are encouraged to bring friends home, and to

participate in after school activities.
- Parents encourage children to date and have boyfriends and girlfriends, and parents are not jealous of children's friends.
- Parents deal openly and easily with their own sexuality and do not confide in the children about sexual issues.
- Parents are available to discuss and explain the children's sexual awareness in appropriate ways.
- Parents do not drink alcohol or smoke marijuana with children.
- Both parents contribute to the well being of the family, the household and the children, and share in financial support, child care, house care, cooking and planning, unless one parent is in school full time, or is sick, or has a child home under age 3.
- Family members sit down together for meals, and spend time together talking, playing, reading, and going out together recreationally, with appropriate separate time for each member according to his or his needs.
- Members do not watch TV addictively (every night) as a baby sitter or to avoid family intimacy. Families watch little commercial TV. Among children, IQ and reading tests show a clear-cut pattern. *The more time spent watching TV, the lower the scores.*
- No one has any addictions—no nightly cocktail hour—nobody gets drunk—everyone communicates instead. This does not mean it is unhealthy for children or parents if parents have a drink *once in a while*, a glass of wine or beer with dinner. It *is unhealthy and addictive* for parents to be high or stoned in the presence of children.
- No one physically abuses *anyone else*—no name calling.
- Parents do not make overt or covert sexual overtures toward children.

APPENDIX

PARENT REPORT CARD

(Adapted from Brown University Family Therapy Newsletter)
For each item, circle the grade your parent has earned this month.

Understands my moods
A   B   C   D   E   F

Gives me enough hugs
A   B   C   D   E   F

Tucks me in bed at night
A   B   C   D   E   F

Lets me act my age
A   B   C   D   E   F

Helps me with my homework when I ask
A   B   C   D   E   F

Is nice to my friends
A   B   C   D   E   F

Keeps my secrets
A   B   C   D   E   F

Helps me look my best
A   B   C   D   E   F

Cooks good meals
A   B   C   D   E   F

Keeps the house nice
A   B   C   D   E   F

Watches TV with me
A   B   C   D   E   F

Listens to my problems
A   B   C   D   E   F

Is understanding when I make mistakes
A   B   C   D   E   F

Tells me they love me even when they don't like something I do
A   B   C   D   E   F

Tries to explain things to me
A   B   C   D   E   F

Doesn't scream at me when angry
A   B   C   D   E   F

Is never violent or abusive
A   B   C   D   E   F

Thinks about me enough
A   B   C   D   E   F

Spends time with me alone
A   B   C   D   E   F

Makes me laugh a lot
A   B   C   D   E   F

Makes the holidays special
A   B   C   D   E   F

Lets me make my own decisions
A   B   C   D   E   F

Respects my different ideas
A   B   C   D   E   F

APPENDIX

Doesn't compare me to anyone else
A   B   C   D   E   F

Helps me make my room a special place
A   B   C   D   E   F

Helps me get up when I oversleep
A   B   C   D   E   F

Treats all the children in the family fairly
A   B   C   D   E   F

Answers my questions about sex
A   B   C   D   E   F

Helps me buy the things I want
A   B   C   D   E   F

Is understanding about poor grades
A   B   C   D   E   F

Says "I'm sorry" after making a mistake
A   B   C   D   E   F

Doesn't keep bringing up the past, and notices when I improve
A   B   C   D   E   F

Has a loving, peaceful relationship with my other parent
A   B   C   D   E   F

Makes me want to be like them when I grow up
A   B   C   D   E   F

Here is a model Contract to duplicate, sign and give to your children. I adapted it from one published by Hayes School Publishing Co., Inc:

CONTRACT

I, _____, promise to complete the following assignment:

by _____. If I do not complete the assignment as agreed, I understand that the consequences will be: _____

_____.

Parent: _____

Child: _____

Appendix C

If you want to combine a vacation, honeymoon or renewal holiday with **Happily Married Forever Relationship Enrichment**, please come to Maui.

You can reach us by

- Telephone: (808) 879-2766
- Fax: (808) 891-2346
- E-mail:tyler@pairsmaui.com.

Visit us at our

- Web Site: www.pairsmaui.com.

Appendix D

NATALIE'S MAUI APPLE PIE RECIPE

Ingredients:
1/4 tsp. vanilla
1 tsp. lemon juice
1/4 c. Cinnamon Cider Syrup* (preferred), or Vermont maple syrup
3 lbs. Granny Smith apples
1/4 c. brown sugar
1/4 c. white sugar
1/8 tsp. salt
2 tbs. cornstarch
3 tsp. cinnamon
1 c. macadamia nut pieces
1 c. golden raisins
1 ten inch round pie pastry, chilled

Preparation:
Preheat oven to 425°. Place cider syrup and lemon juice in large bowl. Peel, core and thinly slice apples, tossing slices in syrup until coated. In a separate bowl combine sugar, cornstarch and cinnamon. Stir to blend. Sprinkle over apples and toss until slices are evenly coated. Mix in nuts. Arrange apples in a 10" diam. x 2" high (1½ quart) ceramic pie dish, mounding them in center. Spoon remaining liquid in bowl over apples. Place 10" pastry shell over apples and tuck excess pastry under, leaving rim bare. Place baking pan or foil on rack below pie to catch drips. Bake 15 min., reduce heat to 350° and bake until pastry is golden and apples are tender when pierced and

---

* You can order Cinnamon Cider Syrup from Williams-Sonoma, P.O. Box 7456, San Francisco CA 94120-7456. PHONE: 1-800-541-2233. FAX: 1-415-421-5153.

juices are bubbly—about 30 min. Place on rack to cool. Serve warm with a slab of Vermont cheddar cheese, or Ben & Jerry's Vanilla or Cherry Garcia® ice cream on top. Whenever you eat Ben & Jerry's ice cream, you can ease your guilt about calories, cholesterol, or dairy allergies by remembering you're contributing to the rain forest and all the other good causes Ben & Jerry help.

It's easy to make, great to smell all through the house, and delicious to feed each other!

—Notes—

Citations to A Course in Miracles

Chapter 1:
   1 W-pII.229.1:Heading
   2 T-16.IV.11:1&2

Chapter 4:
   1 M-9.1:3
   2 T-6.III.3:7
   3 W-pI.25.1:5

Chapter 5:
   1 T-12.I.3:3&4

Chapter 6:
   1 T-25.IV.4:9
   2 P-3.II.7:1
   3 W-pI.5:Heading
   4 T-15.I.8:2
   5 W-pII.281.Heading
   6 T-7.VI.1:4
   7 W-pI.33.Heading
   8 W-pI.32.6:3
   9 W-pI.15.Heading
  10 W-pI.37.2:7
  11 T-3.VI.3:1
  12 T-5.VI.12:1

Chapter 7:
   1 W-pI.187.6:1
   2 T-26.I.3:6

Chapter 10:
   1 W-pII.1.4:1
   2 W-pI.62.2:2
   3 W-pII.289.1:1

Citations to A Course in Miracles (continued)

   4 T-26.IX.6:1
   5 T-29.VII.1:9
   6 W-pI.8.2:1
   7 T-13.VI.2:3
   8 W-pI.181.5:2
   9 W-pI.164.1:2
  10 W-pI.68.3:2
  11 T-13.VIII.1:1
  12 W-pI.rI.55.3:4
  13 W-pI.99.12:5
  14 T-13.VI.3:5
  15 T-1VI.1:1

Chapter 11:
   1 T-13.IV.7:5
   2 M-24.6:4

Chapter 12:
   1 T-21.II.2:3
   2 T-8.III.4:1

Bibliography

Anand, Margo. (1989), The Art of Sexual Ecstasy. Los Angeles: Jeremy P. Tarcher, Inc.

Anand, Margo. (1995), The Art of Sexual Magic. New York: G. P. Putnam & Sons.

Bach, George R., & Wyden, Peter. (1968). The Intimate Enemy. New York: Wm. Morrow & Co.

Berne, Eric. (1961). Transactional Analysis in Psychotherapy. New York: Random House.

Berne, Eric. (1964). Games People Play. New York: Grove Press.

Berne, Eric. (1976). Beyond Games and Scripts. New York: Grove Press.

Bettner, Betty Lou, & Lew, Amy. (1992). Raising Kids Who Can. New York: Harper Perennial.

Bradshaw, John. (1990). Homecoming. New York: Bantam Books.

Casriel, Daniel, M.D. (1981, November). The Principles of the New Identity Process. Paper presented at the annual meeting of the World Psychiatric Association.

Chang, Jolan. (1983). The Tao of the Loving Couple. New York: E. P. Dutton, Inc.

Chapman, Gary, & Campbell, Ross. (1997). The Five Love Languages of Children. Chicago: Moody Press.

Childre, Doc Lew, & Martin, Howard. (1999). The HeartMath Solution. San Francisco: Harper San Francisco.

Chopra, Deepak. (1997). The Path to Love. New York: Harmony Books.

Chopra, Deepak. (1997). The Seven Spiritual Laws for Parents. New York: Harmony Books.

Clarke, Jean Illsley. (1978). Self Esteem: A Family Affair. New York: Harper Collins.

Dusay, John M. (1977). Egograms. New York: Harper & Row.

Drescher, Joan. (1986). My Mother's Getting Married. New York: Dial Books for Young Readers.

Dyer, Wayne W. (1989). You'll See It When You Believe It. New York: William Morrow & Co.

Dyer, Wayne W. (1992). Real Magic. New York: Harper Collins.

Dyer, Wayne W. (1995). Your Sacred Self. New York: Harper Collins.

Dyer, Wayne W. (1997). Manifest Your Destiny. New York: Harper Collins.

Goulding, Mary McClure, & Goulding, Robert. L. (1978). The Power Is in the Patient. (P. McCormick, Ed.). San Francisco: TA Press.

Goulding, Mary McClure, & Goulding, Robert L. (1979). Changing Lives Through Redecision Therapy. New York: Brunner/Mazel.

Heilbrun, Carolyn. (1997). The Last Gift of Time: Life Beyond Sixty. New York: Dial Press.

Hendrix, Harville. (1988). Getting the Love You Want: A Guide for Couples. New York: Harper & Row.

Hendrix, Harville. (1992). Keeping the Love You Find: A Guide for Singles. New York: Simon & Schuster.

Hendrix, Harville, and Hunt, Helen. (1997). Giving the Love that Heals: A Guide for Parents. New York: Pocket Books.

Hite, Shere. (1976). The Hite Report on Female Sexuality. New York: MacMillan.

Hite, Shere. (1982). The Hite Report on Male Sexuality. New York: Ballantine Books.

Jampolsky, Gerald. (1970). Love Is Letting Go of Fear. New York: Bantam Books.

Jampolsky, Gerald. (1999). Forgiveness. Hillboro OR: Beyond Words Publishing Co.

Johnson, Robert A. (1987). Ecstasy. New York: Harper & Row.

Kadis, Leslie. B., & McClendon, Ruth (Ed.). (1985). Redecision Therapy: Expanded Perspectives.

Watsonville, CA: Western Institute for Group and Family Therapy.
Levine, Stephen, & Levine, Ondrea. (1995). Embracing the Beloved. New York: Doubleday.
Lofas, Jeannette, & Sova, Dawn B. (1995). Stepparenting. New York: Kensington Books,
Maddox, Brenda. (1975). The Half Parent. New York: M. Evans & Co.
Moore, Thomas. (1992). Care of the Soul. New York: HarperCollins.
Moore, Thomas. (1996). The Re-enchantment of Everyday Life. New York: Harper Collins.
Muller, Wayne. (1996). How Then Shall We Live? New York: Bantam Books.
Myers, David. (1992). The Pursuit of Happiness: Who Is Happy and Why. New York: William Morrow & Co.
Paul, Jordan, & Paul, Margaret. (1983). Do I Have to Give Up Me to Be Loved by You? Minneapolis: Compcare Publications.
Paul, Jordan, & Paul, Margaret. (1988). From Conflict to Caring. Minneapolis: Compcare Publications.
Pipher, Mary. (1994). Reviving Ophelia. New York: G. P. Putnam & Sons.
Pipher, Mary. (1996). The Shelter of Each Other: Rebuilding Our Families. New York: Ballantine Books.
Pittman, Frank. (1989). Private Lives: Infidelity and the Betrayal of Intimacy. New York: Norton.
Schaeffer, Brenda. (1990). Loving Me, Loving You. New York: HarperCollins.
Schaeffer, Brenda. (1997). Is It Love or Is It Addiction? Center City MN: Hazelden.
Scarf, Maggie. (1987). Intimate Partners. New York: Ballantine Books.
Simon, Sidney B., & Simon, Suzanne. (1990). Forgiveness. New York: Warner Books.

Schwartz, Pepper. (1983). American Couples. New York: Morrow.
Schnarch, David. (1991). Constructing the Sexual Crucible. New York: Norton.
Schnarch, David. (1998). Passionate Marriage. New York: Henry Holt.
Small, Jacqueline. (1982). Transformers. Marina del Ray CA:DeVorss & Co.
Stinnett, Nick, DeFrain, John, & Beam, Alice. (2000). Fantastic Families. Howard Publishing Co.
Taffel, Ron. (1999). Nurturing Good Children Now. New York: Golden Books.
Vissell, Barry, & Vissell, Joyce. (1984). The Shared Heart. Aptos, CA: Ramira Publishing.
Vissell, Barry, & Vissell, Joyce. (1989). Risk to Be Healed. Aptos, CA: Ramira Publishing.
Wallerstein, Judith, Lewis, Julia, and Blakeslee, Sandra. (2000). The Unexpected Legacy of Divorce. Hyperion.
Wallerstein, Judith, and Blakeslee, Sandra. (1995). The Good Marriage. New York: Warner Books.
Welwood, John. (1985). Challenge of the Heart. Boston: Shambala Publications.
Welwood, John. (1990). Journey of the Heart. New York: HarperCollins.
Williamson, Marianne. (1992). A Return to Love. New York: HarperPerennial.
Williamson, Marianne. (1994). Illuminata. New York: Random House.

About the Author and Editor

Natalie Tyler is a civil rights and peace activist, a poet and a psychotherapist who has counseled over 1,000 couples in her twenty-five years of therapy practice. Her articles have been published in the *Official Journal of the International Transactional Analysis Association, Maui News, Maui Voice,* and *Mauiana Magazine.*

Natalie trains and supervises psychotherapists world wide, and she has presented her original ideas at international psychological conferences and seminars in the United States, Canada, Europe, Russia, China, Singapore, New Zealand, Australia and, most recently, at the International Transactional Analysis Association Conference and the Shambhala Buddhist Retreat in Halifax, Nova Scotia.

Natalie speaks extensively on relationships, and she and her co-therapist husband have hosted their own television program about relationships. Natalie and John have seven children and eight grandchildren.

John Tyler was a practicing attorney for 20 years and then took a year off to sail his boat from France to the Caribbean following Columbus' route. He then returned to graduate school to receive his M.A. in psychology specializing in family therapy. He is a Sierra Club hike leader, an environmental activist, and a poet. He loves co-parenting, co-grandparenting, and presenting workshops worldwide with his wife, Natalie.

John and Natalie's poetry has been published in *Maui Muses*. They are officers of Maui PFLAG, they have a book of wedding ceremonies and vows, and they are licensed wedding officiants in Hawai'i. Natalie and John enjoy their close chosen Ohana (family) on Maui.

HOW TO OBTAIN COPIES OF HAPPILY MARRIED FOREVER

You may request copies of **Happily Married Forever** (ISBN # 0-9702381-0-X) from your local bookstore. If unavailable, please use the **ORDER FORM** below, and we will ship your book(s) via United States Postal Service Priority Mail. Note: Shipping, handling, and book prices are subject to change without notice.

- - - - - - - - - - - -Copy, Clip and Mail - - - - - - - - - - -

☐ Please send me _____ copy (ies) of **Happily Married Forever** at $19.95 per copy (HI residents add .04166 tax), plus $3.50 S&H. For each add'l. book up to 6, add $.50 S&H. Inquire about S&H for quantity orders and for orders outside USA. Make checks payable to Natalie Tyler and include payment with your order form.

☐ Amount enclosed: $_____
☐ VISA   ☐ MASTERCARD
☐ NUMBER _____
☐ EXPIRATION DATE _____
☐ Ship order to: (type or print clearly)

Your Name: _____
Address: _____
City: _____
State: _____
Country: _____ Zip/Country Code: _____
Telphone: _____ E-mail _____

☐ Please mail this ORDER FORM and your PAYMENT to:
  Natalie Tyler
  3270 Kehala Drive
  Kihei, HI, USA 96753
☐ Phone: 808-879-0097; Fax: 808-891-2346
☐ For more information about **Happily Married Forever,** go to: **hmf@pairsmaui.com;** website: **pairsmaui.com**